KAFKAESQUE

MAÏA HRUSKA
KAFKAESQUE

TEN GREAT WRITERS TRANSLATE
THE TWENTIETH CENTURY

Translated from the French by Sam Taylor

WILLIAM
COLLINS

William Collins
An imprint of HarperCollins*Publishers*
1 London Bridge Street
London SE1 9GF

WilliamCollinsBooks.com

HarperCollins*Publishers*
Macken House, 39/40 Mayor Street Upper
Dublin 1, D01 C9W8, Ireland

First published in Great Britain in 2026 by William Collins
First published in France by Éditions Grasset & Fasquelle in 2024

1

Copyright © Maïa Hruska 2024
English translation © Sam Taylor 2026

Maïa Hruska asserts the moral right to be identified
as the author of this work in accordance with the
Copyright, Designs and Patents Act 1988

A catalogue record for this book is
available from the British Library

ISBN 978-0-00-876861-4 (hardback)

This book is supported by the Institut français (Royaume-Uni)
as part of the Burgess programme.

All rights reserved. No part of this publication may be
reproduced, stored in a retrieval system, or transmitted,
in any form or by any means, electronic, mechanical,
photocopying, recording or otherwise, without the
prior permission of the publishers.

Without limiting the exclusive rights of any author, contributor
or the publisher of this publication, any unauthorised use of
this publication to train generative artificial intelligence (AI)
technologies is expressly prohibited. HarperCollins also exercise
their rights under Article 4(3) of the Digital Single Market
Directive 2019/790 and expressly reserve this publication
from the text and data mining exception.

This book is sold subject to the condition that it shall not, by
way of trade or otherwise, be lent, re-sold, hired out or otherwise
circulated without the publisher's prior consent in any form of
binding or cover other than that in which it is published and
without a similar condition including this condition being
imposed on the subsequent purchaser.

Set in Berling LT Std
Printed and bound in the UK using 100%
renewable electricity at CPI Group (UK) Ltd

To you, dear G.

Could you pinpoint the most important encounter of your life? To what extent did – does – this encounter seem to you the result of random chance? And to what extent of necessity?

André Breton, *Mad Love* (1937)

We would help man if we could open, if not his eye for the writing of others, then at least his ear for his own language, and make him experience again the meanings that, without knowing it, he brings daily to his mouth.

Karl Kraus, *Die Sprache* (1921)

KAFKAESQUE

Contents

Introduction 1

KAFKA 7
In the Land of the Soviets

KAFKA AND EUGENE JOLAS 27
The East–West Translation

KAFKA AND JORGE LUIS BORGES 45
Two Men in a Labyrinth

KAFKA AND PAUL CELAN 63
The Balm and the Wound

KAFKA AND MELECH RAVITCH 77
What Have You Done to Your Brother?

KAFKA AND PRIMO LEVI 95
The Recurring Nightmare

KAFKA AND ALEXANDRE VIALATTE 113
Make Me Laugh

KAFKA AND BRUNO SCHULZ 135
If Walls Could Talk

KAFKA AND HEBREW 161
The Promised Translation

KAFKA AND MILENA JESENSKÁ 185
A Love of Translation

Epilogue 221

Acknowledgements 229
Notes 233
Bibliography 243

Introduction

We have been celebrating the wrong centenary. The crucial event of the year 1924 was not Kafka's death, which was met with almost total indifference. It was the fact that, in the aftermath of his death, ten writers around the world felt a new sense of mission: to translate him. From that point, Kafka's books took flight beyond the language and beyond the room in which they had been conceived. The year 2024 marked the centenary not of a death but of a rebirth.

Since then, Kafka's name has given rise to a much-misused adjective, while his work has been fetishised and endlessly dissected. So famous has he become that it is hard to imagine a time when he was not on any literary radar. But that time was only a century ago, when he died unheralded and unknown, leaving nothing behind but his will, written in pencil, and a pile of disordered manuscripts. These were his only ID. During his lifetime, his publications amounted to no more than a few short stories. The offices of his first editor, Kurt Wolff, who published *The Metamorphosis* in 1916, were not located at some chic address in Vienna or Berlin, but in Leipzig.

Kafka was so far from the centre of things in so many ways that nobody would have been surprised to discover that he came from Mars. His name and photograph did not appear in any reference books. There were no biographies of him, official or otherwise, nor a bibliography of his complete works. What did he look like? His face is now instantly recognisable; it has even been immortalised by Andy Warhol. In 1924, though, Kafka was still a nobody, his corpus treated with no more ceremony than his corpse. A 'man without qualities', in the words of Robert Musil. Who was he? Silent in life and dead at forty. A German-speaking Czech Jew from Prague, the capital of a forgotten kingdom in an empire that no longer exists. In what language did he write? What did he think about? Was he a communist, a Freudian, a kabbalist? Did he have a family, followers, friends?

His first translators did not concern themselves with these questions. The 'Kafkologists' did not yet exist.

It takes a pioneer to recognise another pioneer. Kafka's first translators were his discoverers. Knowing nothing, or almost nothing, about the man himself, they were content to gather up his work as if it were treasure that had fallen from the sky. They approached it like K, the land surveyor, advancing towards the Castle, wide-eyed with surprise, wondering by which staircase, through which window or door, they might gain entry. They were his prophets, his messengers, *voces clamans in deserto*. It took tenacity to knock at the doors of publishing houses, proclaiming the genius of an unknown writer. As Alexandre Vialatte confided to André Gide in 1931: 'If I talk about Kafka, people will have no idea who I'm talking about. If I add that he's Austrian, and Jewish, and now Czech, they will be wary of this foreigner, but if I also say that he's perhaps the greatest writer of the century, they'll think I'm just some harmless crank.' This is why the early translations of Kafka were almost all published by the same publishing houses as his translators' own literary works: Gallimard for Alexandre Vialatte; Rój for Bruno Schulz; Losada for Jorge Luis Borges; Einaudi for Primo Levi; Schocken Books in Israel and the United States.

In the years since, Kafka's work has been endlessly translated and retranslated into almost every language on earth. His translators are legion. Here, though, I am only interested in the earliest translations, which have the clumsy charm of all first times.

And, like all odd couples – for that is what they are – these translations remain impregnable to criticism. They short-circuit the works that will succeed them: these pairings – Kafka–Borges, Kafka–Jesenská, Kafka–Schulz, Kafka–Levi and Kafka–Vialatte – exist irreversibly. Like all verdicts, like all metamorphoses, these translations are indelible, carved into paper and into flesh. The German philosopher Walter Benjamin said of Baudelaire – whom he translated into German – that any reading of *The Flowers of Evil* incorporated Marcel Proust's earlier reading. This is true too for the reception of Kafka's work: our reading of it now inevitably owes something to those who read it first.

In the decades that followed, the translation of Kafka became a more professional operation. In fact, it became a discipline in its own right. Newcomers would examine and analyse the first translations, leaving their fingerprints all over them. Dictionaries at hand, they would compare them line by line with the original, highlighting every inaccuracy, every misinterpretation contained in the first translations. The French philosopher Jean de La Bruyère wrote that we only truly love once – our first love – since 'the loves that follow are far less involuntary'. The same is true for retranslations: they are far less 'involuntary' than the ones that came before. Ironically, later translators always reproach their predecessors for being too free.

In 1924, no translator took up Kafka's work by chance or because they had been commissioned to do so. It was something they felt compelled to do; a radical, urgent need. The first translators had no time to lose. They worked in a frenzy, swept along by Kafka's words before their life was swept away by something else: blindness (Borges), a fatal fall (Levi), a dive into the Seine (Celan), a concentration camp (Milena, the Russian dissidents), a bullet in the back of the neck (Schulz) or exile (Jolas).

Translation is a job that requires discretion; you must not overshadow the writer you are translating. With the exception of his lover, Milena Jesenská, Kafka did not meet any of his translators. Five of them were victims of the Holocaust. Paul Celan and Primo Levi, who survived the camps, never escaped the trauma of those years. To be more specific, they suffered from survivor's guilt. Perhaps they became translators for this reason: so that they could disappear, withdraw, if only for the length of a translation.

Every translator gives himself, body and soul, to his work. As the Romanian philosopher Emil Cioran wrote in *On the Heights of Despair* (1934), a translation 'preserves a whiff of flesh and blood, and I prefer a thousand times an idea rising from sexual tension or nervous depression to an empty abstraction'. Kafka's first translators knew, deep in the fibre of their being, what it meant to be *transported* from one language to another. A return trip between two shores: the land of the living and the land of the dead; between the land of fiction and the land of reality. Flaubert always liked to remind people: 'Madame Bovary, c'est moi.' The twentieth century gave Kafka's translators every reason to cry out: 'Ich bin Josef K.'

The parallels between Kafka's fate and the fates of his characters and his translators are numerous, tangled and disturbing. Brought together in a Jackson Pollock painting, their paths would look like a single homogenous whole – but this is an illusion. His translators were not all cut from the same cloth. They managed to be faithful both to Kafka and to themselves. Each of them, in their own way, reflected Kafka and, at the same time, projected themselves into his work. It would take a chart as complex as Mendeleev's periodic table to render the singular nature of each encounter.

In the modern periodic table, element number ten is in the top right corner: neon. Isn't this a providential metaphor for ten translators who all moved through the night with Kafka as their only guiding light? *Neon* is Greek for 'new'. Etymologically, it is a new light. Kafka appears to us here *in the light of* his first translators. There are ten of them, like the ten electrons in every neon atom, microscopic fireflies whirling around the same nucleus. Each electron, like each translator, possesses its own autonomous existence. And the same is true for each of the chapters that follow. But they are all caught in the same field of attraction, the force André Breton called 'that indestructible nucleus of the night'.

KAFKA

IN THE LAND OF THE SOVIETS

Even when you're in the prisoner's dock, it's always interesting to hear people talking about you.

Albert Camus, L'Étranger (1942)

The worst is behind the window.

Kafka, Diaries (1922)

KAFKA

IN THE LAND OF THE SOVIETS

In 1953, Franz Kafka's centenary was a big
event. In 1924, his death prompted only
three notices, this year...

Italy itself. From the 1930s, some eastern
volumes in the USSR. In 1965,
on leaving the USSR, with a smile,

a somewhat embarrassing episode was a rumor that
the Italian novelist Alberto Moravia, on
during an interview in Leningrad, went
no answer came. What such a question could have meant
in front of him.

Kafka was not complete
published until in translation of times were explained
still in the form of someone attempting
one, the fringes of the literary sect has not
common in basements and cellars
and until the mid-1960s were some times

In 1883, Franz Kafka's birth coincided with Marx's death. In 1924, his death coincided with Lenin's. In the eyes of the Soviets, this suspicious chronology did not bode well. From the 1930s on, Kafka's books were banned in the USSR. In 1962, in the literary magazine *Novy Mir*, the Soviet writer Viktor Nekrasov recounted a somewhat embarrassing anecdote: a few years earlier, the Italian novelist Alberto Moravia had asked him, during an interview in Leningrad, what he thought of Franz Kafka. 'Who?' Nekrasov had said. 'Kafka? Never heard of him.'

Kafka was not completely unknown in the Soviet Union, but Russian translations of his work circulated only in the form of *samizdat*, clandestine publications, on the fringes of the literary world. These books were printed in basements and secretly passed from hand to hand until the mid-1960s. We know nothing about the earliest Russian translators of Kafka because they did not put their names to their work. Even today, no biographical information about them is available. These translators left no fingerprints. They are like Josef K in *The Trial*, or K in *The Castle*, figures barely identified by a single initial. As for Karl Rossmann (another K), the protagonist of *Amerika*, he leaves behind his name, his past and himself as he travels from East to West.

The self-effacement that the translator traditionally accepted in the West, be it out of vanity or out of deference to the author, meant something else in the East. The translator's discretion was not merely a tribute to the source text, but a survival tactic. Kafka's first Soviet translators are the perfect illustration of a line by the French philosopher Paul Ricœur: 'Translation is equivalence without identity.' Because there was certainly an equivalence between the imaginary fate of Josef K and the fates of his Russian translators. They were all dissolved in absolute anonymity, and it was this that united them.

So, for a long time, the first Russian readers of Kafka, few as they were, believed that his stories were the work of some Soviet dissident publishing under a pseudonym. In 1984, in the catalogue for the exhibition *Kafka's Century* at the Pompidou Centre, the Russian writer Efim Etkind, himself a translator and theorist of translation, exiled in Paris, recalled: 'I read Kafka for the first time in Leningrad, in the 1960s. I thought it was a text written by a Russian author who wished to conceal his real name. It's an astonishing mix of prose and poetry, very similar to Bulgakov, who also blends everyday reality with the fantastical.'

But what did Kafka do to the Soviet authorities to trigger their animosity? What strange power did the censors detect in his works? What motivated the Glavlit – the General Directorate for the Protection of State Secrets in the Press, founded in 1922 – to ban this writer?

At the time of writing, the Glavlit's files, archived in Moscow, were not accessible to me. So I know nothing about the trial of *The Trial*. I am left to picture a group of mustachioed censors leaning over a dog-eared copy of the book, all of its suspect passages underlined. Did one of them dare to acknowledge that there was some sort of parallel between this novel and the purges orchestrated in the Lubyanka building next door? Could one of those comrades have argued – as the French critic Roger Caillois later did in 1946, in response to a French magazine's provocation – that Kafka, 'with the mysterious judges of *The Trial*, with the invisible bureaucrats of *The Castle*, with the nature of their verdicts – unexpected, irrevocable, incomprehensible yet incontestable, one might even say transcendent – was describing nothing other than the Communist Party'?

Tell me whom you have banned and I will tell you who you are. The hostility towards Kafka is just as instructive as the reverence he attracts. This is what unites intellectuals, despots and saints: they tend to exaggerate the harms and the benefits to the human mind of any given work. They grant books a power that they don't actually possess.

Despite this, it would be simplistic to believe that Kafka's works were forbidden in the Soviet Union only because of a thematic affinity with the totalitarian system. Such a charge would have required improbable perspicacity from the censors. Imagine that a communist dignitary were to recognise himself in one of the characters unflatteringly portrayed in a Kafka novel, if he were to admit this to himself: he would instantly cease to be the figure depicted.

The most widely accepted theory is that nobody understood Kafka better than the communists, and that nobody understood the communists better than Kafka. I believe that the opposite is true: Kafka had no desire to know or understand them. And, to paraphrase the writer Sándor Márai, Kafka's first Hungarian translator, nothing irritates the authorities as much as a silence that denies their existence.

It wasn't because Kafka had any special insight into the nature of the USSR's workings that his works were banned there, but rather because his language was too elusive to be assimilated, and therefore translated, into revolutionary prose. The man and his style were hermetically sealed off from the communists' emotional bombast.

Soon after Lenin asked *What Is to Be Done?*, Kafka's protagonists replied simply: 'Nothing.' He did not take part in confrontation. While communism was striving to mould human existence in the service of a single end,

Kafka was calmly demonstrating that there was no end. This was the biggest sticking point for the Soviets: Kafka could not care less about creating a brighter tomorrow.

* * *

Banning a book in the USSR was not easy. It required constant inspections of imports, bookshops and literary magazines. Wouldn't it have been simpler for the authorities to declare that Kafka was a Marxist? Or to transform his work into a critique of Austro-Hungarian imperialism? They pulled off a similar sleight of hand with the Czech satirist Jaroslav Hašek, an anarchist and a contemporary of Kafka, whose *Good Soldier Švejk* (1921–3), quickly translated into Russian, sold several million copies in the Soviet Union.

Kafka's writings didn't specify or attack any particular regime or party, any tyrant or cause. The plots of his books could just as easily take place on the moon: Kafka provided no geographical clues whatsoever. The anonymity of his settings was as important to him as the anonymity of his characters.

As French writer Julien Gracq once quipped: anyone in possession of a key cannot help considering the book they are reading as its lock. It would have been relatively easy to exploit the ambiguity at the heart of Kafka's work, the multiplicity of possible interpretations, in order to shape the narratives to the communists' ends.

Couldn't a Glavlit bureaucrat have argued, quite persuasively, that 'In the Penal Colony' was actually a description of servitude in a capitalist hell? Couldn't he have interpreted *The Trial* as a denunciation of bourgeois justice? Or depicted *The Castle* as the confrontation between a working-class man and the aristocracy? And couldn't he have portrayed Kafka himself as a proletarian hero? After all, Kafka's day job was in accident insurance law: he spent his whole adult life defending the rights of workers injured in factories.

* * *

To gain a better understanding of Soviet logic, it proves useful, as is often the case, to take a detour through Saint-Germain-des-Prés, the headquarters of Parisian intellectual life. In the postwar years, many French intellectuals were transmitters of Muscovite anxieties. In May 1946, for example, a headline on the front page of the French communist weekly newspaper *Action* asked: 'Should we burn Kafka?'

In a sense, these French communists who wished to destroy the writer's work might have been honouring his last wishes. For nobody was more eager for *The Trial* and *The Castle* to be thrown in the fire than Kafka himself.

The newspaper had put Kafka on its blacklist, with its writers regarding his work as emblematic of 'black literature'. What they meant by this was not only that it wasn't red, but that it was demoralising, depressing; that its author was a sombre-faced killjoy. Pierre Fauchery, the newspaper's editor, justified his call for book-burning by claiming that 'society has the right to take defensive measures against a writer if it judges that his activity imperils its essential interests'. Sure, but how could Kafka be a menace to public order from his grave? Fauchery went on: 'His work expresses, in a contagious way, a certain state of social decomposition. [...] By describing manifestly morbid states of mind, it risks awakening or deepening these states in the reader's mind.' In other words, Kafka was banished for the same reasons that Gregor Samsa was banished by his own parents after his metamorphosis: out of fear that his appearance would frighten the neighbours. They were less concerned that their son had been transformed into a giant insect than by the scandal it would cause.

Meanwhile, the French surrealists, who had adopted Kafka as their patron saint immediately after Alexandre Vialatte's translation of *The Metamorphosis* was published in 1928, responded to Fauchery's editorial with a collective declaration of their own, signed by Arthur Adamov, Antonin Artaud and André Breton, among others. How could anyone dare to reproach Kafka for his clear-sightedness, they demanded. 'One must be both blind and stupid to confuse the darkness of a certain existential literature with Kafka's dazzling night. It is excessive, to say the least, to ask men crushed by rubble to pay for damage insurance.'

The *Action* editorial provoked a flood of responses from readers and writers, among them Francis Ponge, François Mauriac, Maurice Merleau-Ponty and Roger Caillois. Their articles on the subject were published throughout the summer of 1946. Not one of them supported the burning of Kafka's books. Michel Leiris pointed out in passing that the Nazis had already tried doing this.

* * *

For the Soviets, Kafka's greatest sin was his sobriety. Whatever the *Action* editorial may have claimed, Kafka was not a sombre writer, but an irredeemably *sober* one: nothing could intoxicate him. Not the revolution, not women, not ideas. Although he grew up surrounded by the ideologies that left such a mark upon his times – National Socialism, communism, anarchism, Zionism, Freudianism – he remained absolutely indifferent to them. His contemporaries' romantic fascination with History – which Georges Perec imagined as wielding a 'big axe'[1] – seemed distant, even ridiculous, to Kafka. The only axe he cared about was the one that could shatter 'the frozen sea inside us': literature. But you can't execute the tsar with a story.

Let us consider, for example, Kafka's elegant diary entry on 2 August 1914: 'Germany has declared war on Russia – Swimming in the afternoon.' Kafka knew how little influence words had upon the world. Better to hold his breath and continue tracing the lines, from one side of his notebook to the other, eyes fixed on the tiles at the bottom of the pool. Over the four years of the First World War, he maintained a correspondence with his sister Ottla. Despite the fact that Ottla's husband was on the Russian front, Kafka made little mention – in his letters or even in his notebooks – of the war or of the Bolshevik Revolution. He was deaf to the rallying cries of his age. Real life was elsewhere. And the same was true for the war: he was neither a tub-thumper nor a pacifist.

From 1918 on, the world around Kafka was reconfigured by a series of treaties, as was customary in that part of Europe where pieces of paper held the power of life and death over nations and their populations (think: Trianon, Versailles, Saint-Germain, Brest-Litovsk). The Austro-Hungarian Empire was dismembered. The first Czechoslovak Republic was brought into existence, and its neighbours – Austria, Germany, Russia and Poland – were all changed beyond recognition. Overnight, the centre of the continent was stripped of the bureaucratic apparatus that had supported the coexistence of fifteen different nationalities. The administrative, judicial, social and political systems that Kafka had known all his life crumbled into dust. In their place appeared the first apparatchiks and the first *apatrides*. The latter were stateless persons, seen as foreigners wherever they went, invisible and indeterminate; undocumented pariahs, regarded by the authorities in the same way that bastard children are regarded by religious communities. The philosopher Hannah Arendt would later describe them as cosmopolitan: people 'with a passport for every country except their own'. People like Josef K, in other words.

Was Kafka such a prophet that the world around him began to imitate his imagination? No, but he was a keen observer: the distance that he kept between himself and the world had made him sensitive to details that nobody else seemed to notice. Kafka didn't need to read newspapers: living in the same apartment as his parents was enough to teach him about self-flagellation and arbitrariness.[2] And, as a worker in insurance and a citizen of two different countries (Bohemia in the Austro-Hungarian Empire and the Czechoslovak Republic) in twenty years, Kafka also had ample opportunity to learn about the world of bureaucrats, offices and factories. He was able to observe how bureaucracy enabled an empire or an employer, however decrepit, to keep going.

In 1906, the German sociologist Alfred Weber, brother of the more famous Max, was the Chief Examiner of the jury for Kafka's doctorate in law at the University of Prague. During this period, the Weber brothers were creating a new academic discipline – the sociology of organisations. This meant studying bureaucracy 'from the inside', i.e. from the point of view of the bureaucrats. Kafka's characters were sociologists too, in their own way. They studied this same bureaucracy, but 'from below', i.e. from the 'external' point of view.[3] K would never be granted access to the heart of the Castle's bureaucratic reactor: this was the novel's conclusion. And a good thing too! the Weber brothers might have replied. The laws that barred the Jews from becoming civil servants would be their salvation, they believed. That way, they would escape enslavement to the machine. This prediction proved overly optimistic, of course, but perhaps it explains, in a very small way, how Kafka eluded all attempts at indoctrination.

* * *

Zionism, anarchism, communism, psychoanalysis, Hasidic Judaism ... Kafka did not believe in anything for long. His diary entry of 23 January 1922 reads: 'As far as I am concerned, there is not a single rule of life that has proved its worth.'

Kafka did not believe in any kind of 'great leap forward'. The only one that interested him was 'the leap out of the killers' ranks', as he called it: in other words, becoming a writer. He repeated – childishly, perhaps – the same message to his girlfriends, his parents, his friends, his employer, his diary: 'I am made of literature, I am nothing else, and cannot be anything else'; 'my job is unbearable to me because it conflicts with my only desire and my only calling, which is literature'; 'everything that is not literature bores me'; 'I hate everything that does not relate to literature'. This was the only point on which he was intransigent. Writing was his North, his South, his East and West, his only source of tranquillity. He marked out the boundary of this territory into which other people were constantly intruding. When his fiancée Felice Bauer asked him why he didn't want to live with her, he replied: '[...] one can never be alone enough when one writes, why there can never be enough silence around one when one writes, why even night is not night enough.' He begged her to understand that a sovereign life is – by necessity – a subterranean life. He demanded the right to withdraw into a cellar, an attic, a bedroom, any space whatsoever as long as he would be left in peace.

Milan Kundera wrote that a novelist demolishes his house, then uses the bricks to build another house: his novel. Montaigne alluded to 'our very own back room, in which we can establish our real freedom, our principal retreat and solitude'. As for Kafka, he demanded both the novel and the living space, along with the right to take refuge in them whenever he wished.

In Czech, as in several other Slavic languages, the word *pokoj* has multiple meanings, all of which Kafka undoubtedly knew, and which would have delighted Virginia Woolf. *Pokoj* means both a room (spatial, residential) and a form of tranquillity or peace (psychological). The *pokoj* is both a topography and a utopia. *Dej mi pokoj*: in Czech, telling someone to leave you in peace is equivalent to demanding a physical space, a place that is yours alone.

In literary terms, the *pokoj* can be defined as elementary cell of the self. The physical place where you write and, if circumstances require, the psychological space that you carry around with you to be redeployed elsewhere. To find a *pokoj* is to gain a precious, precarious certainty: that you will not be disturbed.

The 'room of one's own' imagined by Virginia Woolf was a physical space – defined, even mapped out – that separated a woman from the constraints of marriage and family. The *pokoj* is portable, and it can put down roots, in a place or in the mind. A powerful illustration was provided by Emily Dickinson, who one day invited her young niece to enter her bedroom. Closing the door behind them, the poet took an imaginary key from her pocket and pretended to turn it in the lock. Then, brandishing this fictional key between her fingers, she told the child: 'This is freedom.'[4] She might just as easily have said: 'This is *pokoj*.'

The *pokoj* is the place where we learn to say no, the location in which we refuse to let ourselves be reduced to nothing. In this sense, it is the incubator of all literature. In the *pokoj* – whether physical or psychological – you become "one" only with yourself, or with whomever you have invited. Conversely, anxiety and restlessness can be translated as *bezpokojstvo* – literally, the absence (*bez*) of *pokoj*. The absence of this space is an open door to *disquiet*.

Kafka lived only to write, not for his lovers or his times. He did not want to 'change life', like Rimbaud, nor to 'change the world' like Marx. All he wanted was a *pokoj* where he could take refuge. This was his only commitment: a little monkish, but also extremely perilous.

The *pokoj* constitutes a form of dissidence in itself. Tyrants hate rooms of one's own, just as they hate private diaries. If Kafka was prescient when it came to totalitarianism, it was perhaps because he was able to observe, like Kundera after him, that when an organisation declared itself to be 'like one big family', all rights to secrecy, to integrity, to *pokoj*, were instantly abolished. Kafka had no more desire to reveal the layout of his room than that of his psyche.

Totalitarianism requisitions language and living spaces too. Why? Because it seeks to extinguish all forms of inner life, of which the *pokoj* is the shelter and the reflection. It is only in the *pokoj*, which unites a room of one's own and a language of one's own, that an individual can arrange her freedom.

In his essay 'In a Room and a Half', the poet Joseph Brodsky, born in Leningrad in 1940 but forced into exile in the United States in 1972 (after a similarly forced detour via the north of Russia), describes how, in the communal apartment that he and his parents had to share with other families, he managed to create a small space all for himself where he could write his first books. This 'half-room' – no more than ten square feet, located in a doorway – is now the site of a museum in St Petersburg. How could Kafka ever have accepted being part of the great Soviet household when he already felt like he didn't belong to his own family? Like his character Gregor Samsa, he would lock the door of his bedroom in his parents' apartment, as if he were in a hotel.

Kafka was equally reluctant to inhabit the shared spaces of language and of the city. Zionist Congresses, anarchist meetings, even family meals: all of them made him feel 'seasick on land'. His language was devoid of plurals and exclamation marks.

In *The Unbearable Lightness of Being* (1984), Kundera depicts a scene in which his heroine, Sabina, is hiding in the bathroom one May Day so she can't be dragged out to the parade. Not because Sabina has any problem with the workers on the march. She is simply sickened by the idea of becoming part of a collective, with banners and raised fists, all chanting the same slogan. 'Revolution [only] desires that the people merge with it; in the sense it is lyrical and in need of lyricism,' explains Kundera's narrator in *Life is Elsewhere* (1973). Not only was Kafka incapable of lyricism, but he had an absolute horror of becoming one with anybody else, let alone with his fiancées.[5] How could he possibly become "one" with any single idea?

Kafka was not like Russian poets such as Maxim Gorky, Ilya Ehrenburg or Vladimir Mayakovsky, who were willing to put themselves at the service of the sentimental masses. Nor did he resemble Isaac Babel, the Jewish writer from Odesa who, for a time, embraced a revolution that he imagined would eliminate all nations and borders. None of Kafka's characters – whether in 'A Hunger Artist' or 'Josephine the Singer' or 'The Great Swimmer' or 'A Report to an Academy' or *The Castle* – show any capacity for exaltation or ecstasy, but quite the opposite. As soon as they have to speak in public to galvanise a crowd, they become mute and wish they weren't there. His characters neither champion revolt nor warn against it.[6] They are content to observe and to enter into endless dialogues with people, animals, the law. They emerge from these dialogues at best empty-handed, and at worst dead.

* * *

'A translation is a verdict,' wrote Emil Cioran. But so is the absence of translation. In the 1960s, however, thanks to Jean-Paul Sartre, the first official Russian translations of Kafka appeared in the USSR. It all began in 1962, when Sartre attended the World Congress for General Disarmament and Peace in Moscow. There, he gave a speech with the strange title: 'For the Demilitarisation of Culture: The Relationship between Culture and Politics'.

The Cold War had fixed interpretations of Kafka in black-and-white terms. All over the world, the meaning of his work was being distorted, Sartre explained. The more that the East insisted on suppressing Kafka, the more the West would use his writing to caricature the Soviet system. And by continuing to censor this writer, the USSR was doing the West a favour. 'To whom does Kafka belong, you or us?' he asked. 'In other words, which of us understands him better? Who benefits most from him?' It was becoming embarrassing for the USSR to silence a writer who was revered by communist supporters of the Soviet regime in the West. With this wonderfully twisted argument, Sartre begged the Soviet authorities to translate Kafka rather than punishing his translators. Translating Kafka into Russian was equivalent to restoring his original meaning, like a museum returning an artefact to its country of origin.

Following Sartre's speech, the Soviet authorities approved two translations for *Innostranaya Literatura* in 1964. This magazine (whose title means simply 'Foreign Literature'), founded ten years earlier, gave its readers a glimpse of the books circulating freely in the West. 'In the Penal Colony' and *The Metamorphosis* appeared in its pages, accompanied by a heavy buffer of prefaces, forewords, afterwords, explanations, annotations, asterisks and footnotes, as if to muffle the detonation of Kafka's own words.

* * *

It was not until perestroika in the late 1980s that a complete translation of *The Castle* appeared. In Russian, as in most Slavic languages, 'castle' is translated as *zamok*. In German as in Russian, *Schloss* and *zamok* mean both 'castle' and 'padlock'. Did all these double meanings act as a padlock on Kafka's mind, confirming his fatalistic conviction that the Castle was forever closed to him and his characters?

KAFKA AND EUGENE JOLAS

THE EAST–WEST TRANSLATION

> I grew up, an American in exile, in the hybrid world of the Franco-German frontier, in a transitional region [...] hemmed in by languages and dialects ready to spring at each other's throats.
>
> Eugene Jolas, Man from Babel (1988)

The village of Colombey-les-Deux-Églises has become so famous as the home of Charles de Gaulle and the epicentre of the cult that has grown around the former French president that it is hard to believe that, prior to this, it was also home to the finest underground literature.

Until it was acquired by the de Gaulle family in 1934, the building known as 'La Boisserie' was completely covered in Virginia creeper, with no running water, no electricity and no telephone line. And yet it was here that a certain Eugene Jolas translated Kafka into English for the first time. He moved into the house in 1927 to create one of the most elegant literary magazines of its time: *transition*. Although edited in France, the magazine's language was English and it was printed, sold and distributed on the other side of the Atlantic by the bookshop Shakespeare and Company, which had been opened – in Paris, on Rue de l'Odéon – ten years earlier by Sylvia Beach.

Born in New Jersey in 1894 but raised in Alsace by a French father and a German mother, Jolas worked in Paris as a reporter for the *Chicago Tribune* and other newspapers during the First World War. He would spend his days writing about the exiles of his age: Germans in the United States, French surrealists in New York, Eastern Europeans in London. By night, he would catalogue, edit and translate – with an encyclopaedic compulsion – many different writers who all, in his words, spoke 'the language of night'. Kafka would almost certainly have liked this expression. Beneath this umbrella, Jolas united works inspired by Dadaism, expressionism and surrealism, by the explosion of artillery shells, the interpretation of dreams and the psychology of crowds.

Ezra Pound, Ernest Hemingway, F. Scott Fitzgerald, Henry Miller, Gertrude Stein and James Joyce – there were a large number of Anglophone writers living in Paris at that time. The weakness of the franc against the dollar had made the French capital affordable for a cohort of Americans that called itself, perhaps a little melodramatically, the Lost Generation. These writers weren't fleeing any kind of existential danger, only a social scene in their homelands that they considered too staid, too sleepy. They established a sort of literary colony in exile, with Shakespeare and Company at its centre. They all lived on the left bank of the Seine, and to some extent their cultural isolation mirrored that experienced by Kafka and the other German-speaking Jewish writers of Prague in the 1920s. In other words, they were living in a bubble, feeling simultaneously displaced and at home.

The pages of *transition* were, however, open to writers from around the world. Jolas made his cosmopolitan ambitions clear in his first editorial, calling upon 'American writers! And those of all other countries' to send him their work: 'We believe that, although art and literature are, in many quarters, growing more definitely racial and national in coloring and texture, their appeal is becoming distinctly international.' This was the meaning behind the magazine's title. *transition* published the first English translations of many European artists and writers: Robert Desnos, Jacques Prévert, Paul Klee, Fernand Léger, Kazimir Malevich, René Char, Vitezslav Nezval, André Gide, André Breton … and, of course, Kafka.

* * *

Jolas published his first translation of Kafka ('The Sentence') in the magazine's eleventh issue, in February 1928. He kept elegant company in those pages: Joyce, Léon-Paul Fargue, Pablo Picasso and Comte de Lautréamont. As chance would have it, this first English translation appeared at the same time as the first French translation, by Alexandre Vialatte in the pages of the

Nouvelle Revue Française, whose offices were only a few streets away from those of Shakespeare and Company.

In the following editions, Jolas also translated 'The Married Couple', 'An Everyday Confusion', *The Metamorphosis* and 'Letter to His Father'. In 1932, there appeared 'The Knock at the Farm-Gate', and in 1938 'The Housefather's Care'.

According to several sources, there was a meeting between Jolas and Kafka's close friend, biographer and literary executor Max Brod, arranged by a mutual friend, the German art critic Carl Einstein (no relation to the more famous Albert). We know nothing of what was discussed at this meeting or even the date that it occurred. Brod never mentioned it in his notebooks, and Jolas remained silent on the matter in his autobiography, *Man from Babel*, published by Yale in 1988. As for *transition*'s archives, they vanished during the German Occupation and have never been found.

* * *

Despite, or because of, its avant-garde stance, Jolas's magazine never had a print run of more than four thousand copies. Even so, like many other literary reviews of this period, *transition* represented an important stepping stone towards the world of the big New York magazines and periodicals. In this sense, its name was well earned, since it was not a destination in itself but a stop along the way – a transition from obscurity to fame. Being published in the magazine did not guarantee the author a green card, but it did provide access to a version of Ellis Island where American publishers could spot their future stars.

It was not until *The Trial* appeared in English in the late 1930s that Kafka posthumously made a name for himself in Manhattan. On 18 October 1937, Ralph Thompson, critic for the *New York Times*, wrote a review of the book. Shaken by his reading of *The Trial*, Thompson expressed surprise that the likes of Gide, Thomas Mann and Aldous Huxley had so lavishly praised a writer whose anxieties he regarded as 'demonic'. He described the novel's plot with suspense and precision. However, nothing in this attentive reading seemed sufficient to dent his conviction that Kafka was merely a sort of depressed version of Lewis Carroll. On what the novel meant, he concluded, 'I am afraid that I have not the faintest idea. It is beyond me.'

* * *

Kafka's works returned to America a decade later, almost by stealth. They arrived initially in the suitcases of German Jewish philosophers who were fleeing Nazism: Günther Anders, Theodor W. Adorno and Max Horkheimer from the Frankfurt School, for example, all made Kafka's work the bedrock of their thought.

Naturally, they had all read Kafka in Germany, in the 1920s and 1930s. But they discovered him anew in New York. Kafka seemed to give meaning to the multiple metamorphoses they themselves were going through in their exile: 'Metamorphosis of man, but also of subject, meaning and, most of all, philosophy, which is disfigured by history,' as the French scholar Léa Veinstein wrote in *The Philosophers Read Kafka* (2019). Their geographical displacement was accompanied by a sort of identity crisis. The imaginary meridian that once connected their body and their language to the same place was gradually worn away.

Consider Günther Anders. When he arrived in New York in 1939, this young philosopher still went by the name of Günther Stern. Disorientated, and hobbled by his limited English, he wasn't able to translate his own texts into this new language. Nor did he recognise himself in the translations carried out by other people who were supposedly qualified to do such work. The gulf between his present and his former self grew wider and deeper every day. Like Dostoevsky – who, in *Notes from Underground* (1864), bemoaned his isolation ('I am alone, while they are everybody!') – Stern regretted 'no longer belonging to an us'. His friend Adorno expressed the same idea in different words: 'In German, I write like myself, whereas in English I can only write like other people.' Exile drove them into strangeness and banality at the same time. They were now denied access not only to their home but to their own language. Is it possible to be yourself in such circumstances? Kafka had been surrounded by the same questions.

Exasperated, Stern asked his friends to call him by a different name. In German, the adverb *anders* means 'differently'. Günther Anders now lived in New York; Günther Stern had remained in Berlin. To remain oneself, but with another man's face: this was Dostoevsky's definition of the demonic. Günther Anders doomed himself to wear the same face while going by someone else's name: a reverse metamorphosis.

Like any physical separation, the loss of a language causes a sudden anaesthesia of the five senses. How can you express in a foreign language the nuances of what you hear, see, taste, touch and smell when these sensations do not correspond with known words in your brain? How can this language translate the deepest, most subjective meanings when it is fundamentally alien to you? In the nineteenth century, the German linguist Wilhelm von Humboldt conceived the idea of a *Sprachsinn*, literally 'the sense of the language': the sense that enables you to name and apprehend the other five. Language as the sixth sense. When you are deprived of it, you are not only exiled from the world, but from yourself.

In his *Journals of Exile,* Anders wrote in 1962: 'All of us have known how it feels to stop, one day, in a city, on a street corner, and notice that the things people are shouting, the sounds of the world, seem suddenly addressed only to others. In other words, we have all had the experience of no longer being there.' The English language dried up his thoughts: he felt unable to draw from it the resources necessary to write and think fluently. Not that he was losing his memory of German words – he spoke his native language every day within the Germanophone community of New York – but he and his language now lived only in a tiny, closed circuit.

* * *

In the years that followed, Eastern European intellectuals such as Vladimir Nabokov, Czesław Miłosz, Norman Manea and Joseph Brodsky crossed the Atlantic, fleeing Soviet communism. They had all read Kafka. And since, as Nabokov once wrote, 'Even genius does not save one in Russia; in exile, one is saved by genius alone', they obtained visas for the United States, usually in conjunction with a teaching position at a university.[1] This new category of writer-professor inspired Nabokov's thirteenth novel, *Pnin* (1957), named after its protagonist-avatar who paces the corridors of an enormous college. Pnin goes from department to department, from office to office, from storeroom to storeroom. Like Nabokov, he barely makes enough to survive and lives in a series of sublet rooms. The only space that truly belongs to him is the suitcase that he lugs around everywhere he goes.

In the middle of the Cold War, all these Pnins taught comparative literature in their Slavic accents in the lecture halls of Princeton, Cornell, Bard and Columbia. Milan Kundera, too, was a Pnin: upon arriving in France, he was hired first as a professor at the University of Rennes, then at the School for Advanced Studies in the Social Sciences in Paris: 'I got into a car and drove as far west as possible,' he wrote in *The Book of Laughter and Forgetting* (1978), 'to the Breton town of Rennes, where on the first day I found an apartment on the top floor of the tallest high-rise tower. When the sun woke me the next morning, woken by the sun, I realised its large windows faced east, toward Prague.' These writers, who became bilingual through circumstances, were doubly sensitive to the transports of the imagination, and to Kafka's in particular. And who other than a Pnin, alive to the sufferings inflicted by the passage from one language to another, from native speaker to foreigner, could understand the metamorphoses at work in Kafka?

* * *

How do you remain yourself whilst in exile? By bringing with you what has forged and nurtured you, what has formed and deformed you. 'You have to have in you some cell, some gene, some germ that will vibrate in answer to sensations that you can neither define nor dismiss,' declared Nabokov in his first masterful lecture on *The Metamorphosis* at Cornell. This cell is another manifestation of the *pokoj* that I mentioned in the previous chapter: the *pokoj* makes exile bearable. The *pokoj* is the place where the writer's ink is made, steeped, infused and dyed. The *pokoj* exists prior to any language, before a single line has been written.

Nabokov puts it best:'Ought one not to reject any longing for one's homeland, for any homeland besides that which is with me, within me, which is stuck like the silver sand of the sea to the skin of my soles, lives in my eyes, my blood, gives depth and distance to the background of life's every hope? Some day, interrupting my writing, I will look through the window and see a Russian autumn.'[2] Yes, the *pokoj* is the physical or psychological place into which we wish to withdraw when yearning for *depth and perspective*, sheltered from the noise of the world.

* * *

How could Kafka's books, which his Prague friend Franz Werfel predicted in 1913 would 'never get beyond Tetschen' (Tetschen-Bodenbach being located on the German–Czechoslovak border), how could these books – contemptuously dismissed by the *New York Times* in 1937, so distant from modern America and so antithetical to its tastes – become a mainstay of Ivy League curricula less than twenty years later?

The Pnins constructed their masterful lectures with a key element of their *pokoj*: the books they had read. Not that they were able to emigrate to the United States with shipping containers full of books – those, for the most part, remained in Europe, abandoned, destroyed or confiscated. They smuggled their books to America in a different way: behind their foreheads.

An illustration of this was provided by the Viennese writer Stefan Zweig. In the foreword of *The World of Yesterday*, his memoir written in 1942 in a hotel room on the other side of the planet, Zweig apologised to the reader for writing 'with nothing to jog my memory; I have no copies of my books, no notes, no letters from friends [...] I have nothing left of my past, then, but what I carry in my head. At this moment everything else is either lost or beyond my reach.' Isn't this essentially the same as Nabokov's 'cell', mentioned above?

After being destroyed in 1938, and before being reborn on paper, the 'world' of yesterday existed only in its author's head. Zweig carried this *pokoj* with him to Brazil and he reconstructed it in a room where nothing belonged to him. It is like the two bodies of the king: the *pokoj* is dead, long live the *pokoj*.

And a final example. In *Testaments Betrayed* (1993), Kundera wrote about the Russian-Polish-Lithuanian composer Igor Stravinsky. Did this man – who was born in St Petersburg, composed his most famous works in Switzerland, became famous in Paris, died in exile in New York and was buried in Venice – have a *pokoj*? '[...] his only homeland, his only home, was music, all of music by all musicians, the very history of music;

there he decided to establish himself, to take root, to live; there he ultimately found his only compatriots, his only intimates, his only neighbors.' The Pnins in America were all – each in their own way – engaged in an endless, consolatory, transatlantic conversation with Kafka.

* * *

The French historian Pierre Nora devoted eight thousand pages to *lieux de mémoire*, the 'realms of memory', immaterial and material, which contribute to a population's identity over the course of its history. In these terms, Colombey-les-Deux-Églises represents the ultimate realm of memory. It forms, shelters and reflects, even now, the idea of Gaullism.

The realm of memory, in the sense intended by Nora, presupposes the existence of an *us* and maintains it as such. Or, in other words: this is an official realm.[3] It requires the intervention of public authorities to preserve it, and to draw attention to it.

The *pokoj*, by contrast, establishes the existence of a *me*, and does not involve anybody other than that *me*. It is not public, but amniotic. The *pokoj* provides this *me* with a sense of continuity in spite of the ruptures and inconsistencies that life forces upon it. It is the space in which the disparities between the world of yesterday and the world of today can be patched up, like a metaphysical tailor's shop. Where the different parts of our selves can be accommodated. The *pokoj* can be stitched together from books, lexicons, sounds, notebooks, paintings, scents, memories, fabrics or – as with Nabokov, above – the colours of a 'Russian autumn'. It surrounds, nurtures and differentiates the story that we tell, to ourselves and to the world. There are no two identical *pokoje*.

So what does all this have to do with Kafka and America?

The Pnins taught comparative literature. For them, this was a godsend. What other discipline would have allowed them to speak, semester after semester, about the authors who had given life and shape to their thoughts? In a foreign land, teaching what you know by heart is a way of staying at home, a way of softening your landing. Talking about the books you've read, whether over dinner or in a lecture hall, enables you to exist in a new space, and to furnish that space as you wish. With the help of Kafka, the Pnins were able to walk around the edge of the void, to regain their footing in this new world.

In the classes they taught, the Pnins were careful not to present Kafka as some sort of soothsayer. They did not feel bound by any message dictated by a consumptive twenty years earlier, but they also knew that Kafka had penetrated their world in a way that nobody else ever had. For them, the discovery of Kafka's works, before or after their exile, had been a source of inspiration, a mirror, a springboard, and a source of consolation too. Kafka provided them with the same feeling of relief as a stranger who, despite knowing nothing about you, is able to put into words a vague anxiety that you thought you were the only one to feel.

* * *

When something is familiar to us, we call it 'part of the furniture'. This was how the Pnins felt about Kafka's books. They were an integral part of their inner life: part and parcel of their biography as well as of their bibliography. They knew his work like the backs of their hands. Even with their eyes closed, they could have located the cutlery drawer, the light switches, the creaky floorboards, the envelope full of love letters, the first aid kit, the uneven step that trips the unsuspecting visitor. So it was that in his masterful lecture on *The Metamorphosis*, before speaking a single word to his students, Nabokov would draw a map of Samsa's apartment on the blackboard, sketching the layout of the rooms.

* * *

Kafka never set foot in America. He could, however, imagine all the promises and complications that this land would represent for people like him, lost and alone.

Written in 1909 but published posthumously in 1927 in Berlin, his novel *Amerika* recounts the setbacks suffered by a man named Karl, after his arrival in New York. In the last chapter, there is finally a glimmer of hope: Karl is inexplicably hired by a travelling circus company called the Nature Theatre of Oklahoma. Not only is Karl completely unqualified for this job, but nobody tells him what exactly his duties are. In any other novel, Kafka would probably have described such a situation in nightmarish terms, but as he prepares to embark on another voyage into the unknown, Karl seems serene for the first time since the beginning of the story. Why? Because he has befriended another freshly hired foreigner, Giacomo, who is just as lost and bewildered as he is. Giacomo provides Karl with the same comfort that Kafka would later offer the Pnins: the reassurance that he is neither mad nor alone. They are equally lucid. The novel ends with two beautifully peaceful sentences that could almost have been written by Jack Kerouac: 'So there they sat, the two of them, close together, rejoicing in their hearts over the journey. Such a carefree journey in America they had never known.'

KAFKA AND JORGE LUIS BORGES

TWO MEN IN A LABYRINTH

The writings left behind by those your dread
Implores won't have to save you. You are not
The others, and you see your feet have brought
You to the center of a maze their tread
Has plotted.

Jorge Luis Borges, 'You Are Not the Others' (1976)

It all starts with the Castle.

Kafka, *The Castle* (1926)

The Argentine writer Jorge Luis Borges translated eighteen of Kafka's works into Spanish, and wrote more than fifty prefaces, articles and lectures about him. Indeed, Kafka seems to have permeated Borges' life so profoundly that Borges struggled to remember the circumstances in which he first read one of his books. Sometimes he would date it to his years studying German in Geneva, between 1914 and 1918; at other times he pinpointed 1925, the year in which the magazine *Revista de Occidente*, which he read assiduously, published an early anonymous translation of *The Metamorphosis*.

Edited in Madrid by the philosopher José Ortega y Gasset, *Revista de Occidente* was to the Hispanic world what the *Nouvelle Revue Française* was to the French, or what *Innostranaya Literatura* was to the Russians: a literary weather station. In the 1920s, Buenos Aires was to Madrid what Prague had been to the centre of German literature a few years earlier: both a hive of activity and a distant province. Kafka lived his entire life in the latter city, which was a melting pot of Jewish, German, Czech and – from 1917 on – Russian communities, but he did not identify with any of them. As for Borges, despite his Anglo-Castilian heredity and his Germano-Latin education, he too kept his distance from his many possible identities.

Borges and Kafka both shared a similar regret: not being Jewish enough. Kafka was from an assimilated Ashkenazi family, and he always lamented not receiving a religious education that might have given him a semblance of tradition and belonging to hold on to. This is the main subject of 'Letter to His Father' (1919). Similarly, Borges – who was fascinated by the Kabbalah, about which he wrote several short stories, including 'The Aleph' (1945) – wished that he could have been part of the only people to have chosen the book (with or without a capital B) as their home. So, in 1934, when the nationalist Argentine newspaper *Crisol* wrote that he was suspected of being 'secretly Jewish', Borges responded with a heartfelt and funny article entitled 'I, Jew' ('Yo, Judío'). In that article, he stated that he had sought for a Jewish ancestor, tracing his genealogy back several centuries – in vain. Had he found one, he would have proudly declared his Jewishness rather than keeping it a secret.

To understand what Buenos Aires was like at the end of the nineteenth century, you have to read Santiago

Amigorena's magnificent novel *The Ghetto Within* (2019). Successive tsunamis of Italian, Spanish, French, Russian and Jewish immigrants had transformed the city into a European capital in exile. There, Borges observed the encounters, fusions and combinations – sometimes ill-fated, often incomplete – between cultures, languages, religions and imaginations. In his work, as in Kafka's, these multiplying crossroads became an omnipresent, obsessive image.

The thread that connects Kafka's labyrinth with Borges' is tangled, however, and in more than one place it has been cut completely.

* * *

Borges was a translator before he was a writer. It was his translations that smuggled modernity – via Poe, Woolf, Faulkner and Joyce – into Argentina. He did not start translating Kafka until 1938.

During a conversation with an American academic in 1976, Borges said that he had purchased the complete works of Kafka in 1938 from the bookshop of the Goethe Institute in Buenos Aires. But since 1933 Kafka's books had been banned – and even gleefully burned – by the Nazis. Had someone failed to inform the German bookshop that Kafka was an enemy of the *Volk*, the *Geist*, the *Blut*? Of course, the Reichstag's orders could have taken some time to cross the Atlantic. Kafka himself seemed to predict such a scenario in a short story that was published about twenty years earlier, in 1919, in the magazine *Selbstwehr* (which translates as Self-Defence). In 'A Message from the Emperor', a herald who has been given the task of transmitting a message from an emperor gets lost in the endless corridors of the palace. The series of rooms, staircases and courtyards is so serpentine, so twisted, that he will never deliver the message. The message's intended recipient sits beside their window, as in an Edward Hopper portrait, and waits, forever dreaming of the contents of that lost dispatch. This story is an inversion of *The Castle*: whereas the land surveyor K desperately seeks entry, the messenger is doomed eternally to search for an exit.

'An Imperial Message' dramatises the two boa constrictors wrapped around modern man: his arms are bound by subordination to orders; his legs constrained by the impossibility of grasping the infinite. Like most of Kafka's stories, this one is exceptionally short: less than a page. In a single sweep, it satisfies the two qualities that Borges admired in a literary work: brevity and endlessness. Although the story is but a tiny fragment of Kafka's work, it functions as a microcosm, containing, reflecting and duplicating the greater whole. If the contents of the imperial dispatch are never revealed to its addressee, it is not because of some tragic event (the herald is neither murdered nor struck by lightning) or a lack of determination (the herald is not lazy), but because the messenger is lost in a world for which he possesses no map or compass. 'An Imperial Message' is Kafka as microcosm, containing within it the genetic code for both *The Castle* and *The Trial*: the wait for a revelation that never comes. Each of Kafka's stories is like all the others and yet unique. Their individual patterns echo infinitely within each other.

Kafka exercised an *attraction* over Borges – in both the magnetic and the fairground meanings of the word. Borges constructed his work like a hall of mirrors: not the one in Versailles, but the kind that you can find at any travelling fair. It is here, in a maze of mirrors – where man moves from one perplexity to the next, with the unpleasant sensation that he is going around in circles – that the Borgesian and Kafkaesque universes intertwine.

* * *

Is it possible that the telegram from Berlin ordering the destruction of supposedly degenerate literature somehow got lost over the Atlantic and never reached the bookshop in Buenos Aires? Well, for whatever reason, the shelves of the Goethe Institute remained inviolate. Damned in Berlin, these books came back to life in a shop window, more than seven thousand miles from the pyre to which a tyrant had sentenced them. This was what gave them the halo that Borges so adored.

All the ingredients of a metaphysical tale were here. Firstly, the volume containing the 'complete' works of Kafka was misnamed. According to Max Brod, Kafka got rid of more than ninety per cent of his writings during his own lifetime, and left a will asking his executor to burn the remaining ten per cent after his death. This wish was never granted: from 1925 on, Brod set to work gathering, editing and publishing Kafka's works all over the world.

This unwitting legacy was itself something of a labyrinth, since in none of his notebooks had Kafka given any indication of the intended order of the chapters he had written.[1] Secondly, and this was the detail Borges seized upon to formulate his vision of the translator's craft, Kafka had not finished any of his three great novels – *The Trial*, *The Castle* or *Amerika*. The volume that Borges had purchased from that bookshop was, therefore, a reconstruction, a creature moulded from the clay of the manuscripts that Brod had salvaged. A golem.

Presented in this way, the volume of 'complete works' takes on the appearance of a collection of miraculously saved texts, a miracle squared. Imagine the ecstasy that Borges, with his kabbalistic tendencies, must have felt at discovering such treasure. Kafka's novels were literally endless: not only unfinished, but offering an inexhaustible supply of possible interpretations. And, the infinite is the central preoccupation of the Borgesian imagination – its very cornerstone. For

Borges, all literary work is by its nature work in progress. He hated the word 'definitive' for that reason. After all, who can say of anything that it has a definitive quality? The fact that Kafka's novels were unfinished did not constitute an obstacle, in Borges' mind, but rather an invitation to permanent resurrection. Since the original had not uttered its final word, the story would be continued in translation.

Borges outlined and refined a theory of translation in a series of short essays about his own translations of James Joyce and of *Thousand and One Nights*. His theory: that the relationship between an original and its translation is like a meeting of two incompletions. Both the original and the translation are endlessly perfectible objects. The date of birth of the first does not give it any superiority over the second. The (very Walter Benjaminesque) idea that an original work possesses an 'aura' meant nothing as far as Borges was concerned. Why should the original be considered superior simply because it came first? Far from being diluted, the original became enriched, Borges believed, as its avatars multiplied.

Borges claimed to have drawn this conclusion from his own experience. As a child, he first read *Don Quixote* in English, rather than Spanish, having inherited the book from his English grandmother. 'When later I read *Don Quixote* in the original, it sounded like a bad translation to me. [...] I had the feeling that it wasn't the real *Quixote*.' Not only did he consider the Spanish version inferior to the English, but he thought the original was unfaithful to its translation.

To say of a translation – because it is *only* a translation – that it can never attain the heights of the original is based on the idea (which Borges deemed false) that the original should be considered the definitive version of a work. But, for Borges, the concept of a *definitive* text belonged only to 'religion or exhaustion'.[2]

If we accept Borges' assertion that any original work is doomed to a state of incompletion, then it contains within it the possibility of another version of itself. Every translation embodies a new version of the work that – doomed to being just as incomplete as the original – inspires the following translations, and so on.

Retranslation, based on what Antoine Berman called 'infinite rephrasability', is implicit in the very act of translation. Each translation leaves behind a space for the next one, as if the Tower of Babel was being built as it collapsed.

Borges had no interest in word-by-word translations. If a translation is so faithful to the point that it becomes identical to the original, then it supplants it. A flawless translation is like a crime of passion: it would kill the beloved object. This is why Borges did not advocate for either fidelity or betrayal, but simply for difference: an indefinable element that distinguishes the original from its other versions.

According to Borges' theory, literature, like geology, is essentially sedimentary in nature. In order for the original to endure, its translations must be deposited on top of it, in successive layers. Here, Borges was mirroring a principle outlined by the German mathematician Gottfried Wilhelm Leibniz a few centuries earlier: the identity of indiscernibles. In plain English, the idea behind this principle is that, even if you spent your whole life searching the entire earth, you would never in all of nature find two absolutely indiscernible physical entities. Borges transposed this principle from mathematics to translation.

His short story 'The Parable of the Palace' (1960) illustrates Leibniz's Law in Borgesian terms. It can be summarised as follows: in China, an emperor showed a poet around his immense palace and its grounds: the rooms, the gardens, the pathways, the spectacular views. To thank him for this, the poet composed a poem that translated all these spaces so perfectly into words that it 'brought him immortality and death. [...] Everyone fell silent, and the Emperor exclaimed: "You have taken away my palace!" The executioner's iron sword terminated the poet's life. [...] Others tell the story differently. There cannot be two identical things in the world: as soon as the poet recited the poem (they tell us), the palace disappeared.' Anything that is translated too perfectly ceases to exist.

* * *

The year 1938 marked a turning point: Borges' father died, Germany annexed Austria, the Austrian–Czech border was closed, and Max Brod fled to Palestine, with nothing in his suitcase but Kafka's manuscripts. Now aged forty – the same age that Kafka had been when he died – Borges suffered a severe case of sepsis, which left him hovering on the verge of death for almost two weeks. This episode accelerated the deterioration of an eyesight condition he'd had since childhood. That same year Borges was also hired by the public library of Buenos Aires. 'If I were asked to what has worst affected my life, I should say my father's library. In fact, I sometimes think I have never strayed outside that library.' Nicknamed the 'Library Man', Borges made this place the backdrop to all of his books as well as his preferred living space.[3] He spent his nights there translating Kafka, taking notes, and (as he himself admitted) 'imitating' him. Immediately after this, he wrote three Kafkaesque stories that helped him become world famous: 'The Lottery in Babylon', 'The Circular Ruins' and 'The Library of Babel'. The last of these begins with the words: 'The universe (which others call the Library) is composed of an indefinite and perhaps infinite number of hexagonal galleries, with vast air shafts between, surrounded by very low railings. From any of the hexagons one can see, interminably, the upper and lower floors.'

Where the labyrinth is both a cerebral and metaphorical representation of the infinite, the library is its physical manifestation.

Kafka and Borges were both incapable of tolerating the outside world as it was, with all its inescapable flaws. Literature was their only source of tranquillity, their only habitable space; the only space in which they could find their way. Their only *pokoj*. Karl Rossmann in America, the land surveyor outside the Castle, Josef K before his judges, Gregor Samsa with his parents, Josephine the Singer in front of her audience, even the Great Swimmer on top of the podium that he never climbed: what Kafka's characters all have in common is that they are outsiders who do not understand the rules or the languages of the places in which they find themselves.

The labyrinth is the condition of modern humanity: Kafka and Borges also agreed on this point. The only way to survive it, they seemed to say, was either to go ever deeper within it or to build a counter-labyrinth. For Kafka, this took the form of a 'burrow' that was never quite sufficiently sealed off from the noises of the outside world. For Borges, the labyrinth took the form of a circular library that contained everything it was possible to express in every possible language. 'I am literature and nothing else,' Kafka wrote often in his diaries and his letters. Borges expressed the same sentiment. He was the Library Man. A creature of paper and ink. 'S'enfouir, c'est s'enfuir,' wrote French art historian Georges Didi-Huberman in his essay, *Le Témoin jusqu'au bout*, on the German Jewish linguist Victor Klemperer's captivity during the Second World War, a play on words that can be translated as: *to burrow is to flee*. Kafka and Borges were not fleeing the same ghosts, but they both built their barricades out of the same material: bookshelves.

* * *

Of all Kafka's translators, Borges became his most docile disciple. From 1939 on, the two writers were even published by the same Argentinian imprint: Losada. In the postwar years, Kafka became a publishing phenomenon, in Europe and America – the idol, in turn, of existentialists, surrealists and psychoanalysts. Borges did not want his hero's work to be appropriated by any school or ideology: 'The pleasure to be found in Kafka's work [...] precedes all interpretation and depends on none.'[4] In 1983, the centenary of Kafka's birth, Borges was on a European speaking tour; he repeatedly told his audience how, in his youth, he used to dream of 'being Kafka'. Not of being his double or his clone, but actually being him. 'I wrote a few stories in which I forced myself, ambitiously and pointlessly, to be Kafka. "The Library of Babel" is one of these stories: an exercise in which I attempted to be Kafka. But all I could do was ape Kafka. He was a genius; I am merely a writer.' As in 'The Parable of the Palace', there can be no equivalence between the author and her translator, or between the owner of a palace and its visitor.

* * *

In 1955, when his blindness had turned from 'a slow summer dusk' to almost total darkness, Borges was appointed director of the National Library of Argentina.[5] Surrounded by books he could no longer read: the irony inspired him.[6] Despite his blindness, he was still able to surprise his visitors by moving around the library buildings as if around his own home, without a cane or an assistant to guide him. He impressed people with his detailed knowledge of the library's shelves, from the basement to the ceiling, and the way he would practically jump from floor to floor. The Uruguayan writer Emir Monegal reported having seen Borges whirling up the stairs and running along the aisles whistling. 'I try to follow him, tripping, blinder and more handicapped than Borges because my only guides are my eyes.' Borges had metamorphosed into the creature he himself had imagined in his fable 'The House of Asterion' (1947), who felt at home only in the depths of a labyrinth.

Here we can find the clearest distinction between Kafka and Borges. The two men did not see their labyrinth in the same way. Borges adored the idea that his library represented infinity, and for him it was a source of pleasure. Whereas for Kafka, this same infinity was equivalent to imprisonment. Where Borges blindly strolled through corridors, carefree as a child, Kafka's corridors were like something from a nightmare. Borges loved the fact that the contents of his library were perpetually expanding, that he could never know them all. He didn't care about being lost, about knowing where the entrances and exits were located; all that mattered to him was that the walls of the labyrinth were lined with books. For Kafka, by contrast, the imminence of a constantly delayed revelation, like some lovers' rendezvous that is forever out of reach, was a form of torture.

Let's try to visualise it. If a publisher has to imagine a cover to illustrate the complete works of Borges, he will perhaps turn to the artists Sonia and Robert Delaunay, contemporaries of Kafka, whose paintings depicted multicoloured (Eiffel) towers and circular movements: a joyous form of cubism, with all its rough edges smoothed over. Where Kafka saw only downward spirals, Borges saw concentric circles lined with imaginary bookshelves, surrounding him endlessly, as comforting as the knitted threads of a woollen blanket. In another medium, the Borgesian imagination might also find its artistic form in the work of the Catalan architect Antoni Gaudí, whose masterpiece is the still unfinished Sagrada Família.

This cathedral is also reminiscent of *The Tower of Babel*, painted by Pieter Bruegel the Elder in 1563. The Habsburgs, always quick to embrace irony, acquired it during an era when they reigned over a polyglot empire. An empire that the poet Rainer Maria Rilke, a Prague-born contemporary of Kafka's, described as a 'temporary arrangement that ends up remaining temporary'. What does Bruegel's painting show? Cranes, pulleys and a scattering of bricks on the ground. Inside the tower are vaulted galleries upon vaulted galleries, connected by impossible stairways that lead nowhere. The Sagrada Família, under construction in Barcelona since 1882, resembles Bruegel's painting and embodies an allegory of the Borgesian credo. As Jean Cocteau said of Gaudí's basilica: 'It's not a skyscraper, it's an idea-scraper.'

* * *

But let's return to that German bookshop in Buenos Aires, a city that was home, in 1938, to more than a hundred and eighty thousand Jews. The man who ran this shop, surrounded as he must have been by books, was in some ways the ultimate Borgesian hero. A real hero, if – in contrast to the recipient in Kafka's 'An Imperial Message' – he actually received the message from Berlin and deliberately ignored it. What if Borges was not the only blind bibliophile in Buenos Aires?

This selective blindness on the part of the German bookseller, displaying Kafka's books in the shop window of the Goethe Institute in 1938, is precisely what enabled Borges to purchase them in time, before his own vision deteriorated to the point where it would have been impossible for him to translate them. Could *not seeing* be a way of *seeing more clearly*? It may well be that the German bookseller never received any telegram from Berlin. But I cherish the theory of a German version of Bartleby in the Pampas of Argentina.[7] It pleases me to imagine that Borges' translations of Kafka were made possible by this German functionary who, in 1938, chose not to function: a bureaucrat who had refused his Kafkaesque fate.

KAFKA AND PAUL CELAN

THE BALM AND THE WOUND

I am you when I am I.

                          Paul Celan, 'In Praise of Distance' (1948)

A German-speaking poet, a Jew, a Romanian exiled in Paris: Paul Celan's multiple identities are like a set of Russian dolls, although it's hard to tell how they fit together. Lay them end to end and they form a bridge between impossible shores: between two Europes, between two languages, two chasms, between the translatable and the untranslatable, between death camps and poetry. As the French writer Daniel Oster put it: 'On a bridge, one is always in quotation marks, sometimes in parentheses. The bridge is not entirely of the earth, nor entirely of the air, and its relationship with the water is unclear.'[1] Celan clung to his pen the way a man crossing a bridge might cling to the guardrail during a gale. On the night of 19–20 April 1970, he jumped to his death from the Pont Mirabeau in Paris.

* * *

Before I began writing this book, I knew nothing about Celan, except that Germany regarded him as one of its greatest twentieth-century poets. His most famous poem, composed upon his return from a Nazi labour camp, is entitled 'Todesfugue' ('Death Fugue'). I read one stanza, then two, then three. The original meaning of the word fugue was 'flight' or 'escape'. In Celan's poetry, it is akin to a burial: the voices do not cavort, but are piled up in the ground. 'Wir schaufeln ein Grab in den Lüften,' he writes in the poem: 'We scoop out a grave in the sky where it's roomy to lie'. Like the artist Marc Chagall, Celan imagined floating characters; he called them 'das Volk-vom-Gewölk': 'the people-of-the-clouds', with rhymed alliteration of *Volk* (people) and *Wolk* (cloud). A people whose only cemetery is the sky.

Before reading Celan, I used to see Marc Chagall's paintings as soft, whimsical, childlike creations. I saw upside-down lovers surrounded by musicians and blue goats, all of them floating over flower-filled meadows. And then that image of 'the people-of-the-clouds' destroyed their innocence. Now I see them as wreaths of smoke disappearing above a crematorium.

* * *

Paul Celan was born Paul Antschel (Ancel) in 1920 in Czernowitz. Two years earlier, this city had still been the capital of an Austro-Hungarian province called

Bukovina, before it became part of Romania. Like Celan, the city was known by more than one name: Czernowitz, Cernăuți, Chernivtsi. And, like Prague, Czernowitz changed hands several times: first it was Ottoman, then Austro-Hungarian, then Romanian, then Soviet, and since 1993 it has been part of Ukraine.

Celan grew up speaking the same language as Kafka: German. However, neither of them ever considered himself German. Their Germanness did not reside in their ever-changing passport, but in their language. In 1924, when Romanian became the official language of Czernowitz, the Celan family members did not change their habits. They continued to speak German. This was the language of their *pokoj*. There are more than six hundred miles between Prague and Czernowitz. Despite that distance, the Kafka and Celan families were marooned on the same linguistic island.

In these regions, German sounded impossibly remote. *Hochdeutsch*, or 'high German', represented the language of a country that no longer existed. A 'paper' language, as its detractors labelled it. A language 'without quality', as Robert Musil might have said. Who would want it, now that the 'compact majority' (as Freud might have said) communicated in either a Latin language (Romanian) or in a Slavic language (Russian or Ukrainian)? In these lands that had lost all their Germanness, speaking German suddenly seemed anachronistic, absurd and even suspicious. There was no place for the language or its speakers anymore. Besides, what were they still doing here, these Jewish families, chatting among themselves in German?

* * *

The architects of the Holocaust didn't trouble themselves with such subtleties, but it is worth remembering that at this time there existed in Europe two distinct Jewish worlds. In the East, there were the *Ostjuden*, who inhabited the lands from Galicia and Bukovina (home to Celan) to the Russian Empire, Poland, the Baltic countries, Ukraine and Belarus (home to Chagall). In the West, the world of the *Westjuden*, home to Kafka, included countries that were essentially under Germanic control: Germany, Austria, Hungary and Bohemia.

To further complicate matters, these two worlds were subdivided into several linguistic clans. Orthodox Jews spoke Yiddish, while assimilationists, often nostalgic for the days of Emperor Franz Joseph, the last Habsburg Emperor to rule before the First World War and champion of Jewish emancipation, remained faithful to German, the only language they knew. Between them lay the Zionists, an expanding group who championed neither Yiddish nor German but the rebirth of an ancient language: Hebrew.

For these communities, choosing a language had nothing to do with aesthetic or psychoanalytical whims; it was a matter of political urgency. Each language contained within it the possibility of an 'us'. And each 'us' contained within it the hope of a place where they could live in peace. A substitute homeland. A *pokoj*.

When Kafka first saw a bearded Jew in a black kaftan in Prague, he thought he was hallucinating. What forest could this strange bird possibly have flown from? This encounter was like a Persian encountering Montesquieu: how could one *not* be an *Ostjude*? How could he have lived so long, knowing nothing of this other world? To Milena Jesenská, he confessed being the most western of western Jews.

Kafka became infatuated with Yiddish for a time, took a class in Hebrew, and concluded that German covered reality with a cold, false veil. In October 1911, he wrote in his diary: 'Yesterday it occurred to me that I have not always loved my mother as much as she deserved and as I could only because the German language hindered me from doing so [...] the Jewish woman who is called Mutter therefore becomes not only odd but also foreign.' Convinced that German was scrambling his thoughts, he described himself, in a letter to Max Brod, as a man torn between four impossibilities:

> The impossibility of not writing;
> The impossibility of writing German;
> The impossibility of writing differently;
> The impossibility of writing.

These were, he believed, four dead ends that made a literary career inaccessible to people like him. Too Czech for the Germans, too German for the Czechs, too Jewish for some, not Jewish enough for others. Four times a foreigner, he did not feel at home anywhere, not even in the arms of his *Mutter* with her unlovably Germanic name.

At the time when Kafka was listing these obstacles, the German language had not yet, technically, killed anybody. The unspeakable had not yet supplanted the impossible.

Then came the Holocaust.

Paul Celan's parents were deported in 1942. His father died of typhus, his mother from a bullet to the head. Celan survived two years at a labour camp in Moldavia. When he returned to Czernowitz in 1945, the family home had been repossessed and the doors sealed. History had turned the world upside down; the poet was about to turn it inside out, like a glove. And Paul Ancel would turn the syllables of his name back-to-front to become Paul Celan.

Then came exile. First in Bucharest, then in Vienna, and finally in Paris.

* * *

In the wake of the Holocaust, Theodor W. Adorno, exiled in New York, added another impossibility to the ones Kafka had listed in his letter to Max Brod: writing poetry after Auschwitz. There was no rhyme or reason to this century, and anyone who claimed the contrary was guilty of piling barbarism upon barbarism. Language, like everything else, had been bombed into submission, and nothing remained under the rubble. Celan's response to this was: But Adorno, what else do you want to do, if not write poetry? Although it was true that German was the language of his mother's murderers, 'There is nothing in the world for which a poet will give up writing, not even when he is a Jew, and the language of his poems is German.' For Celan, it was impossible not to write in German, impossible not to write poetry and impossible not to do both at once.

And impossible not to translate Kafka. He began doing so as soon as he returned from the camps. In 1947, the first Romanian translation of Kafka appeared in print: Paul Celan's version of the parable 'Before the Law'.

Celan was a polyglot. In addition to German, he spoke and translated from Russian, English, Italian, Portuguese, Romanian, Hebrew and French. Two of the five volumes of his *Complete Works*, published by Suhrkamp in 2010, are dedicated to his translations.[2] Mandelstam, Apollinaire, Dickinson, Rimbaud, Lermontov, Chekhov, Cioran: he seized upon poets with a reputation for being untranslatable. It may be a stupid question, but why didn't Celan simply choose to abandon German and adopt a different language after the war, rather than wandering like a 'sad poet of the Teutonic tongue'? Surely, among all those other languages that he spoke so fluently, there must have been one that he could have called his own.

But no. None of his other seven languages could seduce him away from the eighth. German was not merely one courtesan in a harem; she was his favourite. Despite all the torments he had suffered at the hands of this language, it continued to pulsate inside him, animating his senses, beating in his blood. 'It is only in one's mother tongue that one can tell the truth. In a foreign language, the poet lies ...'[3] To rebuild the core, load-bearing walls of his existence, Celan could imagine no other mortar than the language his mother had spoken. Not that other languages weren't good enough material. Quite the reverse, in fact: the other languages were so malleable that they would have *given way* beneath the force of his words, like a wall collapsing under too much weight. What Celan wanted was something to lean on, struggle with, bang into, push against. He refused to have the same kind of relationship with his mother tongue that he might have had with a dead language. He wanted, simultaneously, to find himself in his mother's arms again, and to avenge her.

Should Celan have followed his compatriot, Emil Cioran, who 'heroically betrayed' his mother tongue?[4] Like Celan, the Romanian philosopher moved to Paris; there, from 1937 on, he claimed that he had been 'liberated from his own past' by switching permanently from Romanian to French.

Or should he have emulated his neighbour, the writer Aharon Appelfeld? Born in Czernowitz in 1932, he was deported at the age of ten to a concentration camp, from which he escaped. He survived in a Ukrainian forest with the help of other outcasts. Arriving in Palestine orphaned and mute, Appelfeld chose to forget. Nothing remained of his life before the Holocaust: not his parents, or his memories, or his language. He had to forget German so he could become Jewish, he told Philip Roth. This phrase reminds me of another I heard once in a report on members of the Foreign Legion: 'I didn't learn French, I just forgot Russian,' a soldier told the journalist. The polysemy of the word 'forget' in the Slavic languages is worth noting here. In Russian, the verb *zabyt* means 'to forget'. In Polish, Czech and Slovak, it means 'to kill'. This isn't especially surprising. Forgetting wipes away, obliterates and, in the long term, annihilates the most uncertain parts of us. Following the principle of an eye for an eye, I wonder if there are languages that cancel each other out?

The space for tranquillity which I have called the *pokoj*, Celan referred to as the 'meridian'. He explained this choice in detail during a speech entitled 'The Meridian', which he gave when receiving the Georg Büchner Prize in 1960. His meridian could not be reduced to his Parisian apartment, nor to his family home in Czernowitz, nor to the bookshelves of his library, nor to the German language, nor to his circle of friends. His meridian united all of them into a single place: himself. This meridian enabled him to sail the high seas within him. 'The meridian is a kind of homecoming.'

* * *

Between the four walls of home, and even more so between the four corners of his page, Kafka blushed at the idea of making a mistake in German that might betray him as a foreigner in the eyes of his judges – his readers. His language was emphatically unemphatic. It remained on its guard.

Celan took the opposite approach. He composed his poems with the impudence of a man who has nothing left to lose. He promised to 'Jewishise' the German language; to remind it of the vigour and vitality of a world it had sentenced to death. To Adorno, who feared that any attempt at poetry after Auschwitz might sound like 'the musical accompaniment with which the SS like to drown out the screams of its victims', Celan responded that his poetry did not aim to accompany the horror but to reproduce the moans of the dying. An a cappella *Guernica*, without violins or fanfares.

Celan probed the mystery of Auschwitz in the language of Auschwitz. Return to sender. 'I write from within the language of death itself,' he often declared in his speeches, as if to warn his audience that the man standing before them was one of the living dead.[5] Celan invented a linguistic antidote.

Celan's poetry could sometimes seem abstruse, incomprehensible. Primo Levi, who translated Kafka into Italian, was for a long time perplexed by Celan's 'inarticulate babble' and its 'semantic nihilism'. He'd seen enough smoke in Auschwitz; the last thing he wanted was someone to thicken it. Levi considered Celan's 'Death Fugue' to be verbal 'chaos without glimmer of light'.[6] And he was right: that's exactly what it is. The substance and form of the poem is darkness. And darkness has no syntax. If it had a meaning, if people could find their way around inside it, it wouldn't be called darkness.

Levi's *If This Is a Man* (1947) was an attempt to explain the death camps, to translate them in the clearest way possible. His criticism of Celan was that his writings were disjointed, bedraggled, breathless. A scene from *The Trial* offers a metaphorical illustration of this disagreement between Celan and Levi, between poetry and fiction, between the comprehensible and the incomprehensible. While Josef K is waiting to be taken before the court, the policemen – who had arrested him at dawn that morning, with no warning – reproach him for his dishevelled appearance. Why hasn't he dressed more suitably, they ask. Josef K's response could also be Paul Celan's: 'If you accost me when I'm still in bed, you can't expect to find me in my evening dress.'

KAFKA AND MELECH RAVITCH

WHAT HAVE YOU DONE TO YOUR BROTHER?

He would say what he is, before saying what, through the encounter, he has become.

Gaston Bachelard, preface to Martin Buber, *I and Thou* (1938)

There is no one from whom you can learn the truth, not even from me, born as I am a citizen of falsehood.

Kafka, *Investigations of a Dog* (1922)

When the poet Avrom Sutzkever was called to testify at the Nuremberg Trials against Franz Murer – the 'butcher of Vilnius', who had murdered his family – he noted in his diary, on 17 February 1946: 'I want to speak in Yiddish. [...] I wish to speak in the language of the people whom the accused attempted to exterminate. [...] May my language triumph at Nuremberg as a symbol of perdurance.'[1] Ten days later, he testified – in Russian. The court did not recognise Yiddish among its official languages. And even if it had, there was nobody who could translate it, for the very good reason that Yiddish was now almost literally a dead language. The Holocaust had exterminated it along with most of its speakers.

During Kafka's lifetime, Yiddish was still very much alive. While it was German that held together – albeit in a wholly artificial way – the Habsburg Empire, in the same way that Russian held together the tsarist empire, Yiddish was the language that bound eleven million speakers scattered across the continent of Europe, according to Kafka. He had been mesmerised by this language from his very first encounter with it. Yiddish seemed to give life and strength to an entire people, however dispersed it became.

The life of Kafka's Yiddish translator, the poet Melech Ravitch (the pseudonym of Zechariah Chone Bergner), was as scattered as the language itself. Born in Austrian Galicia in 1893, he migrated more than a dozen times, to cities including Vienna, Warsaw, Johannesburg, New York and Jerusalem, before settling in Montreal where, in the 1960s, he translated *The Trial*. Like his friend Isaac Bashevis Singer, Ravitch belonged to a generation of Yiddish-speaking writers who lived on the other side of the Atlantic, depicted by Singer in his novel *Shadows on the Hudson* (1957). They knew that their small readership – those few who had survived the camps – would die along with them. So they were not writing or translating for posterity, but simply for their brothers. When the publishing company Der Kval (The Source) brought out Ravitch's translation of *The Trial* in 1966, the print run was only one thousand copies.

To translate into Yiddish was to face twin oblivions: the disappearance of the language itself and the disappearance of the world that gave rise to it.

* * *

Kafka was no tribune or guru. But on 18 February 1912, at the age of twenty-eight, he went out of his way to organise an evening at the local town hall dedicated to the Yiddish language.

His opening speech was neither lyrical nor learnedly linguistic. Kafka being Kafka, he aimed simply to disconcert his audience.

Before him sat a roomful of Jews from Prague, most of whom considered Yiddish a contemptible language. Was it even a language, in fact? They thought it little more than a dialect spoken by poor Jews from the East. Bereft of grammar or an official dictionary, Yiddish was the antithesis of the German spoken by everyone in Prague. Kafka himself had barely been exposed to this language since Jewish families like his had abandoned the Yiddish dialects of rural Moravia and Bohemia for the German of the big cities. German was now the language of the law, and of those who made it. This equilibrium – in so far as we can call it that – would have remained undisturbed were it not for the Russian Revolution of 1905,[2] followed by the wartime mobilisation of 1914, both of which sparked an influx into Prague of Yiddish-speaking *Ostjuden*.

While Kafka spoke on the stage, in the wings was a troupe of Yiddish actors from Lemberg (today Lviv) and their director Yitzchak Lowy, with whom Kafka had become friends a year earlier. They would regularly perform at the Savoy café-theatre, and it was there that Kafka first heard Yiddish spoken. The chaotic sounds, accents and words of that language breathed new life into his fragile lungs.

* * *

And so Kafka stood, in the middle of this function room, midway between the world of the *Westjuden* in front of the stage and the *Ostjuden* behind it.

He began informing the audience that they would not need subtitles to follow the Yiddish recital. 'Before we come to the first poems by our Eastern Jewish poets, I should like, ladies and gentlemen, just to say something about how much more Yiddish you understand than you think.' In that short speech, Kafka repeated the words *verstehen* (to understand), *verständlich* (understandable) and *Verständnis* (understanding) almost fifteen times. In German, the verb 'to understand' means 'to stand up'. They would understand Yiddish, he assured them: all they had to do was stand up.

'[...] Many of you are so frightened of Yiddish that one can almost see it in your faces,' he went on. Was it because the spectators were afraid of not being able to grasp the meaning of this language, which sounded like some impenetrable gobbledygook? Not exactly. '[...]

Once Yiddish has taken hold of you [...] you will have forgotten your former reserve. Then you will come to feel the true unity of Yiddish, and so strongly that it will frighten you, yet it will no longer be fear of Yiddish but of yourselves.' Kafka sensed that his audience was not fearful that they would fail to understand this language, but that they would understand it all too well.

Marcel Proust had not yet invented *involuntary memory* when Kafka discovered – through his encounter with Yiddish – what we might call *involuntary understanding*. How could the human ear grasp a language it had never learned, let alone had never even heard before? That night, the audience discovered that they had been shaped by a language of which they had no memory. That was what frightened them: Yiddish was a linguistic X-ray, exposing the illusion on which the German-speaking *Westjuden* had based their identity. Yiddish had no need to break and enter the ears of the audience that night: it already had the keys. It was simply coming home.

* * *

Yiddish, said Kafka, was simultaneously intimate, because it was anchored deep within them, and distant, because it had been pushed away. In these circumstances, translation would have been not only futile but dangerous. '[...] Yiddish cannot be translated into German. The links between Yiddish and German are too delicate and significant not to be torn to shreds [...]. If it is translated into French, for instance, Yiddish can be conveyed to the French, but if it is translated into German it is destroyed.'

A translation bridges the distance between two languages. But, according to Kafka, there was no distance between Yiddish and German. In German, the verb 'to translate', *übersetzen*, literally means 'to carry beyond' or 'to take further'. Kafka begged his audience not to put Yiddish at a distance. This language could not be translated for the simple reason that it was not separate or movable. It was not beside or outside, not below or above; it was there, in that room, present inside each of them. Scratch the wallpaper of your *pokoj*, lift up a corner of the carpet, remove a floorboard, look at what is seeping between the layers of paint on your walls: Yiddish.

Kafka here stood in direct opposition to the Goethes, Schillers, Humboldts and other German Romantic thinkers for whom nothing could further enrich a language than its capacity to be translated. Goethe, whom Kafka read assiduously, actually imagined that a language could only emerge greater from the act of being translated: 'The force of a language is not to reject the foreign, but to devour it,' he wrote. Kafka was more clear-sighted: for German, Yiddish would be nothing more than a snack. Yiddish, then, must keep its distance from German if it wanted to survive. After all, German possessed a considerable advantage over Yiddish: it comprised eighty per cent of it. If Yiddish were a company, German would be its majority shareholder. Translate Yiddish into German and you risked destroying all its subtle singularities.

Or, to put it another way, Yiddish and German were like clothes of different colours. If you wash them together, the colours will bleed into one another and everything will end up dark.

* * *

In 1937, the writer – and future Nobel laureate – Elias Canetti went to visit the artist Oskar Kokoschka in Prague. As an expressionist painter in Austria, Kokoschka had been named on the Nazis' list of 'degenerate' artists, and had taken refuge in the Czech capital.

Born in 1905 in Bulgaria (where he stayed for only five years), Canetti now lived in Vienna and belonged to the same Jewish bourgeoisie as Kafka. He had barely set foot in Prague when he found himself transfixed by the sound of the Czech language: '[…] the force with which Czech words hit me might be traced back to my childhood memories of Bulgarian. But […] I had completely forgotten Bulgarian, and how much of a forgotten language stays with us I have no way of knowing. It was certain that in those Prague days various impressions made on me by widely separate periods of my life converged. I absorbed Slavic sounds as parts of a language which touched me in some inexplicable way.' For Canetti, Czech was like a draught of air coming through a half-closed door in a distant room. He thought his Bulgarian childhood was safely locked away, and yet here was a neighbour – the Czech language – come to inform him that it had a spare key.

From the German–Yiddish and the Czech–Bulgarian pairings, Canetti and Kafka drew the same conclusions. They never felt as vulnerable as they did in the arms of a foreign language that seemed to resemble and understand them. The intimacy between two languages does not protect the speaker of those languages, but exposes him to shots at point-blank range.

What is true for the body is true for language. All those thousands of couples who broke up after the Covid lockdown ended are proof, in their own way, of Kafka's belief that being too close is fatal. In 1937, the Spanish philosopher José Ortega y Gasset lamented that, of all the European languages, French was the most difficult for him to translate. Why? Surely French and Spanish are quite similar? Yes, he said, that was precisely the problem. French was too similar, too invasive, offering Spanish no space to paint with its own palette. It condemned the translator to treading water, to the mere tracing of an exact copy. As the French-Lithuanian philosopher Emmanuel Levinas might say: if the other is not elusive, he or she is not *other*. Or, as a couples therapist might put it: the less mysterious a language, the less you desire it.

One last example. Rainer Maria Rilke was – like Kafka – a German-speaking Prague native. He knew the deadly intimacy of Czech and German. In Prague, he wrote, 'the gruesome contact of two linguistic bodies resulted in the inevitable erosion of the extremities of the two tongues'.³ Or, in culinary terms, if you stew two similar languages in the same pot, you end up with an inedible dish. Rilke cursed the Habsburg monarchy for exactly that reason. He reproached them for being so close to the Germanic world that they forgot that most of the Austro-Hungarian Empire that they ruled spread far eastward, and for failing in their duty to preserve the singularity of the Slavic populations. The fusion between languages erases differences without bringing peace. In fact, a philosopher like René Girard would add that this is the ideal breeding ground for violence, because if you are surrounded by such a confused cacophony, the only way to escape it is to create your own *pokoj*. And, if necessary, to take up arms to mark out or defend its borders.

* * *

Roughly half a century after Kafka's speech about Yiddish, it was another language's turn to risk extinction: Czech. Its Russian neighbour could not stop itself, as Milan Kundera reminded us, from 'labelling everything that is Russian as Slavic in order to label everything that is Slavic as Russian'. In 1967, one year before Soviet tanks entered Prague, and not far from the town hall where Kafka delivered his remarks, Kundera gave a speech with Kafkaesque echoes: 'In an empire, a nation can exist and survive only thanks to a language, where the survival of a people finds its refuge.' The empire in question was no longer that of the Habsburgs, but of Brezhnev. In Prague, Russian became the language of the legal system, just as German had once been. People learned it because the government in Moscow forced them to, not out of love or free choice. It was necessary, the Russians said, for the maintenance of *brotherhood* between the socialist republics. Men who were not brothers were nevertheless called brothers. Thus was the groundwork laid: the takeover of vocabulary preceded the takeover of territory.

Where Yiddish was concerned, Kafka was asking for nothing less than protection against German encroachment.

'Be my brother, or I will kill you.'[4] It is hard not to think of Chamfort's epigram when, more than fifty years after Kundera's speech, the Russian president Vladimir Putin orders his Ukrainian counterpart Volodymyr Zelensky to surrender on the basis that Ukraine is 'a brother country' and that Russian and Ukrainian are 'sister languages'. It was not enough to blur earthly borders; linguistic borders had to be dissolved too. In Kundera's novel *The Unbearable Lightness of Being*, set around the time of the Prague Spring, there is a scene in which his character Tereza watches the bodies of women at the swimming pool: 'The women, overjoyed by their sameness, their lack of diversity, were, in fact, celebrating their imminent demise, which would render their sameness absolute.' In that pool, the bodies are, metaphorically, drowned in the mass; they become interchangeable. Vaunting brotherhood between languages with the idea that they ultimately form one single language, like the bodies in Matisse's *Dance* (1910), is destructive idiocy. By sanctifying the family tree of languages with a single trunk and roots, there is a danger of losing sight of the branches' respective singularities. To paraphrase Emmanuel Levinas again, if we focus on the body, we lose sight of the face. And it is my face that, by reminding others that I am at once different and similar to them, makes them less likely to kill me. Without this face, the border between myself and others becomes blurred. The others can then do what they want to me: since there is no longer anything that distinguishes me from them, they can impose their laws on me, without any regard for my own laws.

Slavic languages, Semitic languages, Germanic languages or Latin languages: growing up under the same roof is no guarantee that you will get along. Romulus may have suckled from the same she-wolf as Remus, but that didn't stop him killing his brother.

Such was Kafka's oracular warning to translators: beware the arms that open wide in welcome, for they might crush you in their embrace.

* * *

In January 1912, while he was drafting his speech, Kafka jotted down in his diary that Mrs Klug, one of the actors from the Savoy troupe, had whispered to him: 'I speak every language, but in Yiddish.' Yiddish was a haphazard, makeshift tongue, without declensions or lexicon. Kafka, obsessed by laws, discovered a language without rules: 'The people will not leave it to the grammarians,' he added in his speech. In some ways, you could call it a language of thieves, gathering German, Slavic, Hebrew and Italian words over the centuries and miles. 'Yiddish words retain the speed and liveliness with which they were stolen,' he concluded.

This language was as colourful as the diaspora itself: a sort of Harlequin's coat. It is hardly surprising, then, that Kafka's encounter with Yiddish should come via the theatre. Or, as Victor Hugo put it, via 'the transformation of a crowd into a people'.

Performances in Yiddish grew more common during a period when the Habsburg Empire's big cities were establishing their national theatres. Culture provided an ersatz artillery. So it was out with Johann Strauss's 'Radetzky March' (described by Joseph Roth, author of the novel of that same name, as 'the *Marseillaise* of conservatism') and in with each nation's own canon. In Prague, the Národní Divadlo was inaugurated in 1883 with the performance of an opera by the Czech composer Bedřich Smetana. Even today, we can see the words 'Národ sobě' emblazoned in gilt lettering on the theatre's curtain: 'The Nation – to itself'. At the Savoy café, Kafka witnessed for the first time the sight of Jews representing themselves. For them, the stage offered not only a safe space but the promise of a land of their own.

For its audience, this Yiddish theatre drew all those, like Kafka, who envied the communities of the East the expression of their Jewish identity in everyday life. It was a way of bringing Jews out of the closet. Needless to say, Kafka's new group of friends did not go down well with his father. There was something punk about Kafka knowingly distancing himself from the kind of bourgeois types you might find in Stefan Zweig's fiction. We know from Kafka's 'Letter to His Father' that Kafka Senior considered Yitzchak Lowy to be 'vermin' and did not understand why his son, who still lived under his roof, would want to hang around with such uncouth people. Parental incomprehension ran deep: you slave away to offer your offspring a comfortable life, and those damn kids have the temerity to turn their backs on you for some vanished shtetl and a bastardised language.

Those damn kids were turning in ever greater numbers to the philosopher Martin Buber, who gave speeches to sold-out theatres in Prague. His books, including *The Tales of Rabbi Nachman* (1906) and *The Legend of the Baal-Shem* (1908), had made him a sort of idol among certain citizens who had been deprived of education – or at least access to cultural and religious Judaism – by assimilation. It was a phenomenon that the philosopher Gershom Scholem sarcastically referred to as 'buberty' due to its success with teenagers who wanted to reconnect with a forgotten or never-learned tradition. Buber spoke to the Kafkas of his age: Jews who lived in the centres of cities while remaining on the margins of national and political movements. Kafka never fully entered into Buber fandom, but he did go with Max Brod to hear him speak on several occasions. Born in Vienna in 1878, but raised in Lemberg, Buber spoke about the dilemmas and failures of Jewish existence in Europe. His teachings differed in this way from those of the theologian Moses Mendelssohn who, in the later eighteenth century, had advocated the renewal of Judaism through the opposite means: replacing mysticism with secular knowledge. For Buber, this approach was a dead end: it denied Jews their 'spiritual needs' as well as their 'vocation'. What did he mean by their vocation? Forming a community, of course. Buber believed that, for the world to become habitable, for there to be a *pokoj*, the Jew must have a direct relationship with his neighbours and therefore fully assume the mantle of being a Jew. Because for others to call him 'thou', not the more formal and distant 'you', a Jew first had to start to say 'I' – and vice versa.

Perhaps the appeal of Yiddish for Kafka came down to this: it was a language that spoke to him like a friend, not a stranger.

* * *

As I've already said, what is true for language is true for the body. Buber would have argued that a translation requires the existence of an 'I' that translates, but also – and most importantly – of a 'thou' that will read the translation. A language can be considered living only if it is both desired by a translator and desirous of translations. Demanded and demanding. Without the creation or consumption of literary works, language falls into solipsism. Nowadays, Yiddish is alive only in certain neighbourhoods of Brooklyn, Stamford Hill, Antwerp or Mea She'arim. It has transformed itself into an island to which hardly anyone can berth.

Not even Kafka.

KAFKA AND PRIMO LEVI

THE RECURRING NIGHTMARE

So we are doomed to carry from crib to grave a Doppelgänger, a silent and faceless brother who shares with us the responsibility for our actions, and therefore for all of our pages.

Primo Levi, *Other People's Trades* (1985)

Whenever Kafka read his stories aloud, his friends would laugh and ask him how he came up with such bizarre inventions. Where the hell did he find these stories of cockroach-men thrown away with the rubbish? How could he have imagined such improbable, ridiculous cruelty?

In 1947, when Primo Levi published *If This Is a Man*, an account of his incarceration in Auschwitz, he concluded his introduction by ironically stating that 'It seems to me unnecessary to add that none of the facts are invented.'

Kafka, in his fiction, and Primo Levi, in his memoir, both came up against the same obstacle: their readers' incredulity.

Perhaps Levi feared that people would react the same way that Kafka's friends had reacted thirty years earlier. That, instead of being able to imagine 'what man's presumption made of man in Auschwitz', they would think his story the ravings of a madman. This fear, he wrote, had haunted him since Auschwitz, where, night and day, he and his fellow prisoners all had the same recurring nightmare: that they would survive the camp and go home and, as soon as they began to tell their loved ones what had happened to them, they would be laughed at, not believed. This proved to be a prophetic dream, for it pursued him beyond the camp.

Even though Kafka's stories were entirely invented, his readers still suspected him of absurd exaggeration. During his lifetime, nobody really knew what to make of him: he seemed as far removed from the fantastical literature of the previous century as he did from the artistic avant-garde that dominated his own era.

Levi did not invent anything, but he was likewise suspected of exaggerating. In this way, the gentlemen of the Third Reich hit their target twice over: first, by dehumanising their victims, and then by discrediting them. As Hannah Arendt wrote, the Nazis 'were totally convinced that one of the greatest chances for the success of their enterprise rested on the fact that no one on the outside could believe it'.[1] The Holocaust was conceived with the intention of being inconceivable. In this sense, it was the perfect crime.

After being rejected by a long list of editors, the first edition of *If This Is a Man* was published by a small Turin press called De Silva under the stewardship of Antonicelli and sold less than two thousand copies: a strangely similar fate to that suffered by Kafka. In the years that followed the end of the war, silence reigned. The testimonies of Holocaust survivors and Kafka's fiction – 'In the Penal Colony' in particular – had this in common: what was most disturbing about them was that they did not depict the horror as some aberration or barbaric regression from the norms of modern civilisation, but as the very culmination of modernity, its unspeakable apotheosis.

It was only years later, after various trials including that of Adolf Eichmann, with the dawning of what the historian Annette Wieviorka called 'the era of the witness', that the testimonies of the camps were finally granted some attention. Auschwitz gradually ceased to be inconceivable as the world watched the trials of the men who had conceived it, down to its smallest details, who had dotted its i's and crossed its t's.[2]

By definition, the unimaginable is what cannot be represented by any image. This is why Levi did not include any photographs in his book. He was compelled to create images through the precision of his style and his choice of words. 'If I could enclose all the evil of our time in image, I would choose this image, which is familiar to me: an emaciated man, with head dropped and shoulders curved, on whose face and in whose eyes not a trace of a thought is to be seen,' he wrote in *If This Is a Man*.

In 1915 – thirty years before Levi started writing his book – Kafka experienced the same problem in reverse.

While Levi was unable to convey Auschwitz in anything other than language, Kafka rejected his editor's suggestion that his work should be illustrated with images. It was unthinkable to him that *The Metamorphosis* should be translated pictorially. On 25 October 1915, he wrote a panic-stricken letter to his editor in Leipzig: 'Dear Sir, You recently mentioned that Ottomar Starke is going to do a drawing for the title page of *Metamorphosis*. [...] Not that, please not that! [...] The insect itself cannot be depicted. It cannot even be shown from a distance.'

However talented an illustrator Starke might be, Kafka feared that Starke's drawing would replace his own writing, or worse: that the illustration would kill the insect before the reader could even open the book and picture it. Kafka was convinced that the reader's imagination would only be triggered by the 'unimaginable'.

Flaubert had expressed the same concerns a century earlier. On 12 June 1862, he reacted in a similar way to his editor's suggestion of illustrating *Madame Bovary*: 'Never, while I live and breathe, will I be illustrated, because the most beautiful literary description is devoured by the most pitiful drawing. [...] An illustrated woman looks like a woman, and that's all. The idea is sealed shut in that moment, and all the sentences in the world are useless, whereas a written woman might conjure a thousand women.'

The same logic applies to Kafka's objection: to create a thousand imaginable creatures, the metamorphosis of Gregor Samsa could not resemble any of them.

Kurt Wolff bowed to his author's demands: the insect did not appear on the cover. Instead, for the 1916 edition, Starke drew a man in a dressing gown, turning away from a half-open door, his face in his hands.

Even though he never possessed a copy of that edition, Levi described Auschwitz through that very image: 'In the camps you constantly came up against something unexpected, and that moment of opening a door and finding not quite what you were looking for, but something different, quite different, is quite typical of Kafka.' What both men had glimpsed, each in his own way, was captured by Ottomar Starke's illustration. Kafka's fiction and Levi's non-fiction belonged to the same reality.

* * *

In 1981, before he translated Kafka, Levi compiled – at his editor's request – a personal anthology featuring extracts from the books that had taught him 'another way of saying I'. Entitled *The Search for Roots*, the collection includes, among others, Joseph Conrad, Thomas Mann, Antoine de Saint-Exupéry, François Rabelais and Charles Darwin. Not a single snippet or mention of Kafka, who evidently was not part of Levi's mental furniture. In fact, Levi himself declared that he felt no affinity for Kafka. Levi had endured Auschwitz – wasn't that enough? Why would he choose to relive the

Kafkaesque imagination in the first person? When a journalist expressed surprise at Levi's attitude towards Kafka, he replied that the author of *The Trial* inspired in him a 'repulsion' of a 'psychoanalytical nature'.

True, he was Jewish, like Kafka.

True, he came from an assimilated bourgeois family, like Kafka.

True, his career, like Josef K's, had been interrupted by a sudden arrest.

But Levi insisted that they had nothing else in common. 'We had very different fates. Kafka grew up in very serious conflict with his father; he was the product of three intermingled cultures, Jewish, German and the culture of Prague. He was unhappy in his emotional life, frustrated in his work, and in the end seriously ill. He died young. I, on the other hand, despite the episode of the *Lager* [camp] which marked me deeply, have had a different life, a less unfortunate life.' And, if that was not enough, he added: '[…] I love and admire Kafka because he writes in a way that is totally unavailable to me.'[3]

But, as Hegel observed, the self and the other always meet in the end. So, in 1982, one year after these Kafkaphobic declarations, Italo Calvino, who was working as an editor at the publishing house Einaudi, asked Levi to retranslate *The Trial* into Italian. And he agreed.

Yes, to *re*translate it – because Levi was not Kafka's first Italian translator. In fact, he was the third. I hope you will forgive me for flouting my own rule. The first

Italian translation of *The Trial* was written by Alberto Spaini in 1933, and published by the Torinese editor Franco Antonicelli. Yes, the same Antonicelli – founder of the De Silva publishing house – who had published the first edition of *If This Is a Man* in 1947. As with Levi's account of Auschwitz, that first version of *The Trial* sank like a stone. It has to be said that 1933 was not the most propitious of years. But was there something wrong with this version? At worst, Spaini had smoothed out too many of the original's rough edges, thought Levi. It was an excessively polished, polite translation, guilty of protecting Italian readers from the harshness of the German language. A second translation, by Giorgio Zampa, was published in 1973: Levi judged it one too literal.

Hence Calvino's argument: Levi would be the perfect translator, since neither of the two translations in existence were truly in accord with Kafka. One was pitched too high, the other too low; neither ever hit quite the right note. Calvino could have quoted French writer Jean Giono: 'We live the words only when they are the right ones.' According to Calvino, nobody but Levi was capable of grasping the rightness, the accuracy of Kafka's work. He was not suggesting replacing one text with another, but scoring a new musical arrangement. Kafka–Levi–*The Trial*: not since Maurice Ravel composed *Piano Concerto for the Left Hand* for Paul Wittgenstein (who had lost his right hand during the First World War) had there been such a fiercely tragic trio.

This project was the start of a new Einaudi collection: *Scrittori tradotti da scrittori* – 'writers translate other writers'.[4] These duos seemed so prestigious, and so obvious, that they would discourage future retranslations. What translator would dare criticise Levi's translation of Kafka? Or Umberto Eco's translation of Gérard de Nerval? Or Claudio Magris's translation of Arthur Schnitzler? Or Calvino's translation of Raymond Queneau? Or Pier Paolo Pasolini's translation of Aeschylus? Or Antonio Tabucchi's translation of Fernando Pessoa? Each of these translations grasped the power of the original as never before; each could, in a way, 'break history in two' (as Nietzsche would say). Kafka seemed to have translated Levi in advance, so now Levi would return the favour by translating Kafka.

Actors will sometimes talk about a *dream part*, especially if a director has written a character with them in mind. Of course, Kafka did not write the part with anyone in mind; and, for Levi, it turned out to be more of a nightmare.

* * *

Not only did Kafka create a new language to describe the world, he also invented a new punctuation: he put question marks where there had never been any before. 'Why' is the word that keeps emerging from Josef K's mouth throughout his long trial. And the same is true for K the land surveyor during his numerous interrogations, for Gregor Samsa after his transformation, and for Karl Rossmann as he travels through America. Kafka's characters do not expect any recompense for their misadventures, only an explanation for what is happening to them. And to each 'why', they are all given the same response: such a question has no answer here.

Levi made the same observation at Auschwitz when a guard brutally snatched away an icicle that he was using to quench his thirst. When Levi asked 'Warum?' the guard replied: 'Hier ist kein Warum' – 'there is no why here'. There were no explanations in a concentration camp. And yet Levi kept asking the question, at least to himself. In his mind, the why of the scientist blended with the why of Job. In Kafka's work, the why of the lawyer blended with all the whys of a child.

Josef K knew nothing about the crime of which he was accused: why him? Primo Levi didn't know why he deserved to survive: why him, rather than someone else? He couldn't get over getting out. 'I found myself implicated in the character of Josef K. I accused myself, as he did.' They both reproached themselves for existing. One day, a pious but tactless friend told Levi this theory: if Levi had been spared, the friend argued, it was because God had decided that he should be.[5] In other words, Levi had been saved in both meanings of the word: both physically and divinely. He had been chosen, in part to testify and in part to translate, on behalf of those who had died. Levi could not agree with this convenient definition of providence. To Levi, this way of thinking was not only absurd, but intolerable.

Both Levi and Josef K felt the shame of still being men. The final scene of *The Trial* describes the execution of Kafka's protagonist by two impatient gentlemen. They wonder who will deliver the first blow to the prisoner. Held to the ground, Josef K 'now knew it would be his duty to take the knife as it passed from hand to hand above him and thrust it into himself'. Levi recounted a similar experience in *If This Is a Man*. Dragged to a corner of the Buna laboratory in the Monowitz concentration camp, he remembered: 'I [was] not even alive enough to know how to kill myself.'

* * *

Levi worked on his translation of *The Trial* during the summer of 1982. He had learned certain rudiments of German during his doctorate in chemistry at the University of Turin in 1941; the rest he had picked up at Auschwitz. It was from this hybrid soil, mixing scientific German with barked Nazi commands, that Levi's translation of Kafka would grow.

Because, in order to obey the orders and prohibitions bellowed by camp guards, you first had to understand them. On several occasions, Levi compared the Lager to Babel, with the tower taking the form of a watchtower: 'The confusion of languages is a fundamental component [...] everyone shouts orders and threats in languages never heard before, and woe betide whoever fails to grasp the meaning.' Levi observed that the prisoners with no knowledge of German – in other words, almost all of the Italians – died shortly after their arrival. Misunderstandings were severely punished. There was a clear paradox here, in that learning the language of death increased one's chances of survival.

Levi, who had worked as a chemist before the war, resumed his work fairly soon after the war. He found a job in the 1950s that sometimes took him to Germany on business trips. The way he spoke the language surprised his German counterparts. 'I realised then that my pronunciation was coarse, but I deliberately made no attempt to soften it; for the same reason, I never had the tattoo on my left arm removed.' Levi noted ironically that he had learned German the way other men might learn Italian in a brothel. Kafka's 1919 short story 'In the Penal Colony' features a baroquely cruel camp where machines equipped with ink-dipped needles carve each prisoner's sentence into his flesh. Levi emerged from his own penal colony with a tattoo on his forearm. But Auschwitz had also left its mark on his diction – a sort of verbal tattoo. In Russian, there is a word that is not easily translatable: *osvoit*. The official translation is 'to master', but it is derived from the personal pronoun *svoi* (my), so in fact this Russian verb implies that 'mastery' of something must occur through its appropriation. To genuinely master an object, a place, a language, you must make it your own. Make a place for it inside you. Incorporate it – literally – until it becomes part of your own body. Levi didn't merely learn German; he absorbed it.

In 1923, Kafka wrote this line at the bottom of a page of his diary: 'We are digging the pit of Babel.' What pit? And who is 'we'? The more he dug, the less he knew about what made a man.

* * *

In 1959, Levi was shocked to receive a letter informing him that a German publisher by the name of Fischer had just acquired the translation rights to *If This Is a Man*.

His book had attempted to render, in Italian, the horrors of Auschwitz. Could the language of Auschwitz render the testimony of an Italian? This idea did not inspire him with confidence. Had the German editor bought the rights to salve his own conscience? Levi feared that the translator would mutilate the text by cutting any passages that struck him as unbearable or too shameful for future readers.

What Levi didn't know was that he and Fischer actually belonged to the same 'camp'. The family owners of Fischer Bücherei were Jews of Hungarian origin, who had been dispossessed of their publishing house by the Nazis before it was returned to them after the war.

During Levi's long correspondence with his translator Heinz Riedt,[6] he realised that this project would give the onerous memory of Auschwitz back to the Germans. Of the German translation, he wrote: 'More than a book, it should be a tape recording.'

The publication of this translation galvanised Levi. He felt like he was winning a battle against German denialism: 'I had written the book in Italian [...] but its true recipients, those against whom the book was aimed like a gun, were [...] the Germans. Now the gun was loaded.' As his biographer Myriam Anissimov pointed out, only fifteen years had passed since the liberation of the camps: the Germans who had worn uniforms back then were still alive.

By contrast, the publication of his translation of Kafka in Italian in the spring of 1983 left him feeling empty, helpless, defenceless. Of all the translators studied in this book, Levi was the only one to express regret. 'It's a pathogenic book,' he told a journalist when it came out. 'I felt attacked by this book. [...] It pierced me like an arrow, like a spear.' The process of translating Kafka led Levi to understand his initial hostility towards that author's work. This hostility was not literary or aesthetic in nature, but physical. He felt threatened by Kafka as by a '[...] like the prophet who tells you the day you will die'.

Levi translated *The Trial* at home – 75 Corso Re Umberto, in Turin. This was the apartment where he was born, grew up and remained through adulthood. He left it only once, and not by choice: when he was deported to the camps at the age of twenty-five. After the liberation of Auschwitz, Levi naturally went back to his old home. It was within these walls that he wrote *If This Is a Man* from the notes that he had secretly scribbled – and then destroyed – during his captivity. In a 1979 interview, three years before he started translating Kafka, Levi explained that he owed his moral and physical survival after the camps to the miraculous fact that he had not lost his family or his home.

Philip Roth, who visited Levi in Turin for a long weekend in the autumn of 1986, provided an attentive description of the writer's study for the *New York Times Book Review*: it was comfortable, quiet, tidy, and, like his writing, 'simply furnished'. In this *pokoj*, though, Roth did note one particular detail: 'an unobtrusively hung sketch of a half-destroyed wire fence at Auschwitz'.

Levi had to invite Kafka into his *pokoj* to translate him. The tête-à-tête between the two men lasted a year – the same length of time as his captivity in Auschwitz. The experience plunged Levi into a state of depression that he couldn't escape. 'My defences collapsed as I translated him,' he admitted. The translation destroyed the partition walls that Levi had erected between Turin and Auschwitz, between his life as a man and his life as a non-man. He moved through his translation as if driving along a road at night. Kafka's headlights blinded him. The swerve that followed proved fatal. According to the coroner's report, Levi ended his life on 11 April

1987, throwing himself from the third floor of his spiral staircase.

Translating Kafka had stripped him of all semblance of tranquillity. Had it demolished the walls of his *pokoj*?

* * *

'Our language lacks words to express this offence, the demolition of a man,' Levi wrote in *If This Is a Man*. Here is another paradox: you can demolish a man with words, but you cannot rebuild him with words. Language is at once judge and jury; it's a rigged trial.

Kafka, too, knew that the destruction of a man begins with words. After all, it is not the apples that his father throws that kill Gregor Samsa, but the words spoken by his sister Grete, who one day declares that he is no longer a brother, no longer a son, not even a man.

KAFKA AND ALEXANDRE VIALATTE

MAKE ME LAUGH

He was in love with the preposterous. He hunted it constantly, everywhere. And found it.

Jean Dubuffet, about Alexandre Vialatte,
Jean Dubuffet et le grand magma (1988)

Kafka would soon be crushed under the weight of commentaries, and commentaries on commentaries. We would end up believing that Kafka is the scientific name for a special form of leprosy or some complicated religion. [...] Kafka is, first and foremost, an artist. And it is the artist in him that we speak about least. We have suffocated the artist in favour of a dark thinker.

Alexandre Vialatte, *La porte de Bath-Rabbim* (1953)

A husband and father. A Catholic from the rural Auvergne region. A portly pétanque champion. No algorithm would have thought to match Alexandre Vialatte with Kafka.

The men seemed worlds apart, but their respective biographies do find at least one point in common: their deaths. Kafka died in 1924, Vialatte in 1971, but neither death provoked any kind of fanfare. Their passing was met with identical indifference. The first lines of Vialatte's biography, written by his friend Ferny Besson, read: 'On 3 May 1971, French literature lost one of the greatest writers of our age. Few people noticed. Most of the French population was completely unaware of his work or even his name.' Reading this, it is hard not to connect it to the obituary of Kafka written by Milena Jesenská half a century earlier. 'Dr Franz Kafka, a German writer who lived in Prague, died the day before yesterday – [3 June 1924] – at the sanatorium of Kierling, close to Vienna. Few people knew him here because he walked his path alone, terrified by life.' Does a shared obscurity increase the chances of two people meeting? Kafka and Vialatte refused to network and shunned the limelight, which made them both admired and unknown. The reasons for their respective anonymities had one common element: neither of them was ever interested in joining the kind of clique that might have given them a passport to literary fame. According to Vialatte, this was an enviable position: 'The people who don't know you cannot criticise you, and the few who read you are your friends.' Elias Canetti once wrote that Kafka had 'a passion for making himself insignificant'. It seems only right that, among his translators, there should be at least one 'notoriously unknown writer', as Vialatte described himself.

As we know, Kafka published only a few short stories during his lifetime, throwing away the rest of his writings or, on his better days, leaving them at the bottom of a drawer. Vialatte, likewise, published only a handful of novels. Not because he threw his drafts in the fire, though. His correspondence with his editors Jean Paulhan and Gaston Gallimard shows that, while Vialatte's mind was always filled with ideas for novels, most of them remained fragments. Vialatte was torn between his translations and his devotion to the literary genre that he practised to perfection: journalism. He wrote thousands of articles, for almost as many different periodicals. Charming and delirious, they earned him a small army of devoted fans, who would cut his articles out of newspapers, collect them and exchange them with fellow connoisseurs.

* * *

Vialatte's vocation began with a journey to Germany at the age of twenty-one. It's the kind of journey that we frequently see in Kafka's works. In the opening lines of *The Castle*, a land surveyor from who-knows-where arrives in an unknown village and attempts vainly to understand how it functions. Similarly, Karl Rossmann, the protagonist of *Amerika*, leaves Europe for New York without any idea of what to expect. And in a very short and little-known story called 'The Departure', the narrator sets off, in response to a mysterious calling, without any particular aim in mind. 'Where are you going?' asks his servant. The narrator's only response is: 'Away from here, that's where I'm going.'

Vialatte lived for a long time in the shadow of the Puy-de-Dôme volcano, not of some castle rising above the town. Born in Magnac-Laval, he moved from Brive-la-Gaillarde to Le Puy-en-Velay to Ambert; in other words, from small French town to small French town, far from the convulsions of central Europe. In 1921, armed with a degree in literature from the university in Clermont-Ferrand, he worked as a school monitor and, in his spare time, wrote articles for various student magazines, about anything and everything. This was how he came to be picked up by Jean Paulhan, the publisher of the *Nouvelle Revue Française* and a talent-spotter for Gallimard. Paulhan recommended Vialatte to his friend Bernard Zimmer, who was editing a new bilingual magazine in Mainz called *La Revue rhénane*. Founded a year earlier by the French government, the magazine's aim was to encourage artistic relations between the Germans and the French in the wake of the war. 'I'm not sure he has much to say, but he says it with style and he has the potential to do great things in the future,' Paulhan wrote in his recommendation. Vialatte accepted the job offer and moved to the Ruhr for six years. Only one thing was off limits: talking politics.

Vialatte had had no direct experience of the war because of his young age, and felt no antipathy towards Germany. He had learned German in school, wore square glasses and a bow tie, and possessed the kind of curiosity that is usually the work of foreigners and children. These qualities gave him entry to worlds inaccessible to the spies and diplomats who roamed the country in this fertile, predatory period.

Vialatte told the story of how he discovered Kafka many times. A century later, it has lost none of its mystery. It was the winter of 1926 and he was twenty-five years old, living in Mainz, when he received an anonymous parcel. 'Snow was falling. The postman opened the door. He looked like a Christmas tree – a real German postman. He looked like Bismarck and laughed like an ogre. You would have sworn he had founded the German Empire himself. Yes, a founder, that was it; he seemed like the kind of man who founds something. With one hairy hand, he placed a parcel the size and thickness of a brick on my table. What monument was he planning to build? What was the significance of this first stone? I opened the parcel. It was *The Castle* by Kafka.' Imagine the brick in question: five hundred pages, the title inscribed in gothic letters, and a dust jacket with a photograph of the author. He didn't know at the time that this face would soon represent a destroyed world: that of German-speaking Judaism in central Europe. The portrait showed a man with his tie askew, a half-smile playing on his lips. At first Vialatte thought he was looking at Jean Cocteau. He knew nothing about this man – Franz Kafka – not even the fact that he had died a year before, and that someone named Max Brod had taken on the task of publishing his (unfinished) books, one by one. So it was that Vialatte was served his translation warrant one winter morning, just as Josef K received his arrest warrant, without knowing anything about who was behind it or their motives.

Vialatte's stay in Germany came to an end in 1928, with the almost simultaneous publication of his first novel, *Battling le ténébreux*, by Gallimard, and his translation of *The Metamorphosis* in the pages of the *Nouvelle Revue Française*. Thus was born a sort of literary centaur:

half-novelist, half-translator. From that point on, Kafka became Vialatte's 'companion', 'penal colony' and 'perpetual amusement' for more than thirty years. *The Trial* and 'The Burrow' appeared in 1933, *The Castle* in 1938, *Amerika* in 1946, 'In the Penal Colony' in 1948, 'The Great Wall of China' in 1950, and *Letters to Milena* in 1956. Vialatte wrote roughly a hundred articles, prefaces and letters about Kafka, which have been compiled in a single volume in French by Éditions des Belles Lettres. The book reads like a ship's log, in which Captain Vialatte records the ups and downs in his relationship with this writer, whom he lugged around with him everywhere he went, even as he feared getting too close. Flaubert had warned him: 'Do not touch your idols: the gilding sticks to your fingers.' In Paris as in the Auvergne, Kafka's work was at the very centre of Vialatte's *pokoj*, becoming for him 'a sort of childhood memory, as unforgettable, undeniable and ineffable as the hieroglyphs on the wallpaper at my old Aunt Octavie's house'. Can anyone ever emerge unscathed from such an intense cohabitation?

Vialatte's posthumously published novel, *La Maison du joueur du flûte*, perhaps shows the Kafkaesque influence more than any other: a photographer, locked out of his house, realises that he is incapable of photographing his own home. The pictures he takes are all blurred or badly framed, and he is left with no choice but to pace around his house like K pacing around the Castle: 'I lay siege to my own house [...]. I am the slave of my property.' We can sense Kafka's presence in Vialatte's work in the same way. He is never completely in the frame, and you can never quite tell where one begins and the other ends.

* * *

Vialette experienced a state of enchantment during his first weeks in Germany. He walked around, moved by everything he saw and heard, from 'the charm of diminutives in the Swabian dialect' to 'the pleasures of a Tyrolean folk dance'. It's like reading a cross between Madame de Staël and G. K. Chesterton.

Things started to go wrong in 1924. Not because of Kafka's death – which, as we know, went pretty much unnoticed – but because of the publication in Germany of a book entitled *Mein Kampf*, which gave the first hint of the genocide to come. Monetary inflation was followed by verbal inflation. The German language grew fat on lyricism, losing touch with truth in the process. Kafka's diction, so sober and ascetic, offered a striking contrast. But there were fewer and fewer people in Weimar, Mainz or Berlin who could appreciate, or even understand, that kind of German. Kafka's writing resembled that photograph of him on the book's jacket: lean, lively, agile.

La Revue rhénane avoided contentious subjects. No politics, they had said. And yet politics contaminated everything: how could you describe a play, a book or an evening out without becoming aware of the vile words that insinuated their way into the culture? Writing about a reform of higher education, for example, Vialatte reported discreetly that 'the German university has remained one of the citadels of nationalism, where foreign languages, physics and botany – eminently peaceful sciences – are studied with the aid of a large sabre and a small kepi'. As Germany's madness grew, this climate of threats and warnings made Vialatte feel as if he had a bad case of déjà vu. In a letter to his friend Henri Pourrat on 28 October 1927, he wrote: 'I feel as if I am living in a Kafka novel.' The oddities of German life that he had once taken pleasure in observing now reeked of death. It was time to go home.

* * *

Since he wasn't Jewish, didn't live in Prague, didn't work for an insurance company and didn't have tuberculosis or an unhealthy relationship with his father, Vialatte did not share any of Kafka's sufferings. And he didn't want to focus on them. 'Who exactly was Kafka? I always tried not to know him, to make him mysterious to myself. Why speak about him? Why take from him the prestige of being known only as the author of a strange, unique, brilliant body of work?' All Vialatte cared about was the book he held in his hands: Kafka's words, not his habitat. Forget Prague or Judaism or overbearing fathers or frustrated fiancées or office life. Vialatte dragged Kafka out of his small world and gave him access to a certain kind of universality. By paying less attention to his biography, he found new humour hidden inside his work. Was this why Kafka's humour struck him as more salient than the author's other qualities?

Vialatte also translated Friedrich Nietzsche and Bertolt Brecht: German writers who, though far from cheerful, possessed a kind of fierce wit. In France, Vialatte was probably the first person, if not the only one, to believe Max Brod's assertion that Kafka used to make his friends laugh with his stories about a man who woke up trapped in a cockroach's body. Vialatte saw the funny side of the Kafkaesque.

So he did not understand the gloomy exegeses that grew around Kafka's work in the postwar years. Writers such as Maurice Blanchot, André Gide, Jean-Paul Sartre and Albert Camus – the literary kings of their age, next to whom Vialatte was a nobody – projected onto Kafka all sorts of affinities with the isms of their times. It began with the existentialists, who saw in Kafka a herald of their philosophy, or a dramatisation of their own experience. But that particular version of Kafka – disguised as some professor of despair – was utterly foreign to Vialatte. Why had they made him wear that wig, and that moustache? Go clean up your face, Franz, and then come back. Vialatte felt perhaps the same torment suffered by the creator of the Golem. In Prague, at the end of the sixteenth century, went the legend, Rabbi Loew made a creature that came to life only when he inserted a magical word under its tongue. One night, the creature left Loew's attic, and the rabbi lost all control over it: the Golem roamed the streets of the city. Kafka was, in some ways, Vialatte's Golem: he spent decades translating him in his attic. His words brought Kafka to life in France. He breathed his voice into him, and with it an existence. But this did not prevent the creature getting away from him. Now his Golem was roaming the streets of Saint-Germain-des-Prés. Everyone saw Kafka at their door. 'They changed him. I thought I was launching a prince of humour, but they turned him into a king of darkness.'

* * *

Who is Mr K? Nobody. Everybody. For Vialatte, this gentleman could only be an 'animal in a trilby who waits for the number 27 bus at the corner of Rue de la Glacière'. Himself, in other words. For it was there, in Paris, on the corner of Rue de la Glacière, in an apartment with a view of the local prison, that he moved with his wife and child in 1934. It was a neighbourhood of mental institutions (Sainte-Anne), railway stations (Gare de Lyon, Austerlitz, Montparnasse), monasteries (Cluny) and catacombs (Denfert). Vialatte found this enchanting, and an endless source of inspiration for his articles. Kafka, for his part, often compared his office to a prison. The insurance company offices where he worked for fourteen years, from 1908 to 1922, were located in a luxurious building in the centre of Prague, which is now a hotel. And if you go there and visit room 214, which, according to the hotel map, was once Kafka's office, and open the curtains, you will be unsurprised to find that you have a view of a cul-de-sac.

Vialatte envied Kafka his gift for transforming the 'mildest personal problem' into a 'parable of the human condition'. And yet he himself did exactly the same thing, in article after article. It could be a board game: guess the quotation – Kafka or Vialatte? Diarist or journalist? Take this line by Vialatte: 'Life has become rational. Man has retaken his place as a creature crushed in a nightmare that is, occasionally, brightened by a small joke shop.' That could easily be a Kafka quotation. Or a Sempé cartoon.

A second's distraction and you could lose your footing: modernity eluded both men. Another reason to dwell on it. Office life, for example: Kafka hated every minute he spent in that noisy, crowded anti-*pokoj*. And yet he couldn't escape it, because the office took him away from literature at the same time as it supplied him with it. He tried to explain this paradox to Milena in a letter dated 31 July 1920: true, his office was an 'excessively arbitrary and stupid' place, but some of the things that happened there were so strange that they 'were more fantastical than stupid'. It was as if monotony, through repetition, became mesmerising. Work kept his belly full, but it also replenished his imagination. Vialatte loved writing articles for the same reason: even the most banal event would be shot through with incongruity. 'I don't see anything that isn't fantasy. Least of all reality,' he wrote to his friend Ferny Besson.

Take *The Metamorphosis*: the title misleads the reader about the real plot twist. In the story, Samsa spends only a few minutes thinking about his new condition as an insect.[1] The surprise of waking up with antennae on his head soon fades in favour of a more pressing concern: how will he make it to work on time? How will he update his employer? As Camus wrote, 'we never cease to be amazed by the lack of amazement'. This, in fact, is the true plot twist: Kafka did not consider strangeness as something strange. In this way, his writing marked a clear break with the authors of the previous century. Tellers of fantastical tales such as Gautier, Gogol or Poe conceived strangeness as the culmination of some sort of magic spell. The supernatural appears out of nowhere, cutting the story in two and causing havoc in the characters' neat and ordinary lives. Kafka inverted this idea.[2] In his work, strangeness constitutes a starting point and a backdrop. It's as if he's saying: the monstrous is part of your everyday life – get used to it, because it's not going to get any easier. Whether you wake up with a headache, a beetle's carapace on your back or handcuffs around your wrists doesn't really matter. All these disruptions proceed from the same non-event, Kafka tells us. In other words, there is nothing more natural than the supernatural. For him, the monstrous is not a deviation from legality or normality. On the contrary: the monstrous obeys the same laws as the non-monstrous. And laws are like people: they can adapt themselves to anything. Including monsters.

* * *

In the winter of 1945, Vialatte went to Lüneburg, in Germany, to witness the trial of the Bergen-Belsen camp officials. In the world of before, the main attraction in this small town near Hamburg had been the childhood home of the poet Heinrich Heine. Arriving by train in this country where he had not set foot in fifteen years, Vialatte noted: 'You don't dare look at a chimney smoking anymore. You find yourself holding your breath, afraid that you will inhale humans.'

The Bergen-Belsen trial was one of the first to happen after the war. Its organisation bore no resemblance to the more famous trial of Adolf Eichmann, which would be broadcast all over the world sixteen years later. The hearings took place in Lüneburg's municipal sports hall, which had been converted into a courthouse. Week after week, rubbing shoulders with two hundred other reporters, Vialatte translated for French readers what they could not see, hear or imagine. He was no longer translating Brecht or Kafka or some Rhineland poet, but the language of the Third Reich. He sent his articles to the editors in Paris, and one day he added this warning: 'All the words you will read in this article were spoken by human beings superficially similar to any other human being. Hearing them with your own ears, it is not just Lüneburg that you look at differently, but humanity itself.' Vialatte strove to reproduce the black humour of the dialogues he witnessed. He drew no moral conclusions from this material. To recount such dark events in an equally dark tone would, he thought, have shown a lack of taste. As an elegant man, Vialatte knew how to dress a text: never tone-on-tone. Describing evil in all its fantastical, Kafkaesque aspects was his way of taming it and, perhaps, warding it off. One example occurred during the October 1945 hearing in which the camp commandant Josef Kramer, aka 'the Beast of Belsen', attempted to earn the court's mercy by congratulating himself for founding an orchestra for the camp inmates. The only way Vialatte could deal with this information was to turn it into offbeat humour: 'Just because you're about to get gassed doesn't mean you can't play a nice bit of saxophone!' Vialatte drew his inspiration from the blurred line between tragedy and comedy. Kafka had educated him perfectly. One day, after attending another hearing, he wrote to Henri Pourrat in the Auvergne: 'All this is crazy, tragic, inconceivable, and appallingly comical.'

Sixteen years later, in Jerusalem, Hannah Arendt would illustrate her theory of 'the banality of evil' by describing Adolf Eichmann looking pitiful and skinny in his charcoal-grey suit. In Lüneburg, Vialatte saw only chubby-cheeked chaps who felt confident that they had been doing the right thing. None of the accused appeared haunted by the enormity of their crimes; these men slept soundly at night. They all described their acts as though they were 'simply a joke, a forgettable farce'. Things were not much more encouraging beyond the gymnasium. 'Lüneburg's tranquillity seems utterly undisturbed by the Belsen debates.' Neither the man in the street nor the housewife at home understood or seemed affected by this sudden gathering of journalists in the centre of town. 'What a lot of fuss over a few Jews!' one of them said.

Vialatte realised that day that if Kafka had felt so guilty about everything, it must have been because he had glimpsed a future where nobody would feel guilty about anything.

In October 1945, Vialatte wrote one last article before leaving Lüneburg. He dedicated it to a character who had, until this point, been anonymous and invisible despite being there for months: the translator. In fact, the Bergen-Belsen trial, prosecuted by the Allies, had been conducted entirely in English. The translator, whose name nobody could remember, had been solely responsible for communications between the British judges and the German audience. It was his duty to avenge the dead, and to make sure that the accused understood the fate that awaited them. It was the translator, not the presiding judge, who announced the sentence in German. I am going to reproduce Vialatte's laudation in full here, because it merits our interest: 'It is [the interpreter] who dominates the microphone. It is thanks to him that the full splendid meaning of the words recklessness, deceit and monstrosity is conveyed [...]. It is he who renders the characters, he who grabs the men in the dock as if they were insignificant bits of wood, who dresses them in their answers, emphasising a fold, accentuating a detail, who disguises them as themselves and tosses these puppets to the public. It is he who reveals and amplifies them. I would even dare to say that it is he who creates them, because he makes them larger than life. The whole trial, with all its tragedy, is encompassed in this intelligent voice, in its authority, in its artistic talent. Some people asked me if it would be him translating because they only wanted to attend if he was there. In short, the interpreter is an Arabian storyteller. It is through him that the story happens.'

It is through the translator that the story is born, be it, in Lüneburg, in Paris, everywhere. Those final sentences unwittingly foreshadowed the furore to come. A quarter of a century later, some people would reproach Vialatte for telling a story of his own.

KAFKA AND ALEXANDRE VIALATTE

* * *

In April 1920, upon discovering that his translator Milena Jesenská was spending whole nights working on his stories, Kafka – who had been desperately trying to think of an excuse to write to the young woman – sent her a letter of feigned outrage: 'If you waste as much as one minute of your sleep on the translation, it will be as if you were cursing me. For if it ever come to a trial there will be no further investigations; they will simply establish the fact: he robbed her of her sleep. With that I shall be condemned, and justly so. Thus I'm fighting for myself when I ask you to stop.' In 1974, more than half a century after Kafka predicted that a translation of his work could end up in court, Vialatte proved him right. But the trial took place in Paris, and the translator (who was by this point dead) was accused not of insomnia but of inaccuracy.

A brief summary of the facts: under the terms of a contract signed in 1969, Vialatte granted Éditions Gallimard the exclusive licence to publish all his Kafka translations as part of the leather-bound Bibliothèque de la Pléiade imprint. Following Vialatte's death in 1971, the publisher allowed himself to be convinced that these translations were imperfect, biased, unfaithful. The translator had sinned. It became a matter of urgency to cleanse the translations of all impurities.

(We might note in passing that nobody could find anything negative to say about Vialatte's translations of Gottfried Benn, Bertolt Brecht or Friedrich Nietzsche. The inaccuracies concerned only Kafka.)

Translation is a serious business. Please step aside, and leave this to the professionals. A new translator, a Sorbonne professor named Claude David, was given the task of correcting the translations. Vialatte's rights-holder, his son, opposed this, partly on the basis that his father's moral rights were protected by the law. The court delivered its verdict on 25 September 1974. It did not rule on the accuracy or otherwise of the translations, but only on how they should be published. It was decided that Vialatte's translations would remain intact, but that they would coexist, in the same volume, with David's corrections. Each of Vialatte's mistakes would be highlighted with unerring erudition. A *critical* apparatus, as they call it. An apparatus that, had it been able to speak, would have sent Vialatte to stand in the corner and think about what a naughty boy he'd been. Perhaps the most important thing was to bring this unknown, uneducated nobody from the Auvergne down a peg or two. After all, what gave him the right to have been the first Frenchman to discover Kafka's genius?

'For three hundred pages, you feel as if you are desperately trying to climb a slippery slope, with each step forward taking you back to your starting point': Vialatte's analysis of *The Castle* for *La Revue rhénane* in March 1927 is a brilliantly prophetic description of the form that the Pléiade edition would take half a century later. Here, the reader herself becomes the land surveyor: to work out what could or should have been the correct translation, she is doomed to keep flicking between the text itself, translated by Vialatte, and David's line-by-line corrections in an annexe.³ This edition has often been compared to a labyrinth. Personally, I prefer the more princely analogy of the Château de Chambord. During the Renaissance, King Francis I of France commissioned Leonardo da Vinci to design a double-helix staircase for his Loire Valley hunting lodge. This design enabled two people to use the stairs simultaneously – one going up, the other going down – without ever encountering each other. Vialatte and David rubbed shoulders within the same residence – and the Pléiade edition is surely the most palatial home a writer or translator will ever know – without once making eye contact.

'Man is but dust, which shows the importance of a feather duster,' wrote Vialatte. Likewise, publishers (or their marketing departments) like to present every new translation as dusting off the previous one. In France, Kafka was retranslated as if they were cleaning up a crime scene, carefully erasing all trace of Vialatte's presence. But is it really reasonable to expect a translator to walk into a text only after burying his identity papers, throwing his keys in the Seine, removing his clothes, going through a decontamination chamber, donning a hazmat suit, and leaving his genius in the changing room?

If translation is like a piano piece for four hands, it is also an activity that takes place within four walls. The translator translates from his *pokoj* what another writer has written inside his. Neither works in a state of weightlessness: they write inside a *pokoj* cluttered with the detritus of a life that anchors their words to a body, an era, to the paper on the walls. No matter how timidly he attempts to shrink himself, the translator cannot 'evaporate into impalpability', as the Marquis de Sade fantasised for his novel *La nouvelle Justine*. Expecting transparency from a translation, or from a translator, is as naive as expecting your lover to be an angel. And as the philosopher Blaise Pascal – another native of the Auvergne – once wrote: he who strives to be an angel inevitably ends up behaving like a beast.

KAFKA AND BRUNO SCHULZ

IF WALLS COULD TALK

If art's purpose was merely to confirm what had already been established, it would be pointless. Its role is to plumb the depths of what has no name.

Bruno Schulz, *Letter to Stanisław Ignacy Witkiewicz* (1934)

Kafka was translated into Polish not long before Poland ceased to exist. His translator was named Bruno Schulz. Originally a visual artist, before becoming a writer and then a translator, Schulz published his translation of *The Trial* in 1936. Born in 1892 in a town with a strange name and an unstable spelling – Drohobycz or Drohobych – Schulz grew up on the main square in the centre of town where his father, Jacob Schulz, ran a haberdasher's shop (as, incidentally, did Kafka's father in Prague). During the First World War, the Russians invaded Drohobych and destroyed the Schulz family's home. Young Bruno went to Lemberg to finish his schooling, before leaving for Vienna in 1918 to study fine arts. However, his classes were cut short by his poor health, and in 1924 – the year of Kafka's death – he accepted a job teaching arts and crafts at the secondary school in Drohobych.

The town was subject to what the poet Joseph Brodsky called 'the change of Empires': it passed from hand to hand, or rather from handcuffs to handcuffs. Located in Galicia, a region annexed by the Habsburgs in 1772, it briefly became Ukrainian in 1918, then Polish between 1919 and 1939, then part of the Third Reich, then the Soviet Union, before once again becoming part of Ukraine in 1991. 'Everything that happens here happens only once and is irrevocable. This is why such weightiness, such heavy emphasis, such sadness inheres in what takes place,' says one of Schulz's characters in a short story entitled 'The Republic of Dreams' (1936), in which Drohobych appears anamorphically.

Schulz lived his whole life in Drohobych. Unlike Kafka, though, who felt imprisoned in the 'claws' of Prague,[1] Schulz had no desire to live elsewhere. Drohobych was his anchor, his workshop, his one and only *pokoj*. Here, and here alone, was his imagination able to ferment; it was the only place where he could breathe. Drohobych was for Schulz what Prague had been for Kafka: at once the canvas of his life and the secret backdrop to his work.

* * *

Kafka was a foreigner everywhere, especially in Prague. Schulz was also a foreigner everywhere, except in Drohobych. He left the town only for those brief periods of study in Lemberg, Vienna and Warsaw, and for a three-day stay in Stockholm. The one time he truly escaped his home town was in the summer of 1938, when he went to Paris to show his paintings. It was a strange time to make such a journey, in the middle of the *Anschluss* crisis. It is not clear to biographers how Schulz managed to travel from the east of the continent to the west and back again, carrying his canvases, without being stopped by Nazi customs officials. He took a series of night trains to Paris, passing through Warsaw, Berlin, Aachen and Brussels. He spent three weeks in a hotel on Rue de l'Abbé-Grégoire, in the sixth arrondissement – very close to the Hôtel de la Poste on Rue de Tournon, home to another Galician writer, whom Schulz admired: Joseph Roth.[2] We don't know if the two men ever met, but it seems likely that Schulz's paralysing shyness prevented him approaching his idol.

Despite the storm clouds gathering over Poland, Schulz did not stay long in Paris. He went home to Drohobych as planned. His writer friend Witold Gombrowicz did things very differently. Invited in 1939 to take part in the maiden voyage of a Polish transatlantic liner that sailed from Gdynia to Buenos Aires, Gombrowicz boarded the ship with a small suitcase, never imagining that this would be the last time he saw his homeland. He learned about the invasion of Poland when he arrived in Buenos Aires. Having planned to stay in Argentina for twenty-four days, he ended up there for twenty-four years.

Despite living in Drohobych, teaching in Drohobych and using Drohobych as the setting for his fiction, Schulz was nevertheless considered a great European writer. In Gombrowicz's *Polish Memories* (1959–61), he wrote: 'There were three of us: [Stanisław Ignacy] Witkiewicz, Bruno Schulz and me, the three musketeers. [...] Out of the three of us, Schulz was the most European artist, the most worthy to sit in the circle of Europe's highest intellectual and artistic aristocracy.' Schulz wrote from Drohobych, but not *for* Drohobych. He wrote for an imaginary public, who did not expect him to imitate the Western avant-garde nor to be the ambassador for an eternal or mythical Poland. Like the trapeze artist in Kafka's short story, 'First Sorrow', Schulz was a man clinging to his language and his village as to the two bars of the trapeze. He would launch himself from one and catch hold of the other. In the story, the trapeze artist never descends to earth to salute the audience: he remains perched up high. Schulz clung to Drohobych wherever he went. It hardly mattered to him whether the ground beneath his feet was Austrian, Polish, Russian or Ukrainian: he executed his aerial acrobatics, sheltered from ill winds by the roof of his *pokoj*.

Take Maupassant: did he ever write about anything other than the Pays de Caux? Of course not. His characters leave Normandy no more often than Schulz left Drohobych. That doesn't make him any less great a writer. And if, as Flaubert – another Normandy native – stated, 'Yvetot is just as good as Constantinople', then

Drohobych was just as good as Manhattan or Paris. Schulz defined Poland as 'an anonymous country that belongs to nobody'. This line reframes Alfred Jarry's famous quote from *Ubu Rex* (1896) – 'It takes place in Poland; that is to say, nowhere' – as a stroke of luck rather than a curse. For Schulz, this young land, born in 1919, was like a blank canvas. Unlike his fellow artists, Jews and non-Jews alike, who fled Poland to escape 'the form', or mould, it imposed on them, Schulz felt no need to leave his homeland. He could free himself from the weight of Poland without crossing its borders, because no belonging, no filiation, no *kitsch* (as Milan Kundera would later put it) had a net large enough to catch him. As with Kafka in Prague, Schulz was able to distance himself from the world, to create inside his *pokoj*, without moving an inch.

* * *

The drawings that Schulz made in the 1920s and 1930s – later gathered into a collection, *The Book of Idolatry* – were an integral part of his work. They are like a cross between Helmut Newton's photographs and Francisco Goya's Black Paintings. In these fetishist adoration fantasies, Schulz portrays himself as a trembling little gnome, crawling from some forest, tongue lolling in the presence of haughty, whip-wielding countesses. It's said that these drawings were designed to illustrate an edition of

Venus in Furs (1870), the novel by Leopold von Sacher-Masoch, who lived in Lemberg. Is it possible that one of Schulz's sketches made its way to Prague? More precisely, to Gregor Samsa's bedroom? In the opening paragraphs of *The Metamorphosis*, we learn that on the wall of the insect-man's bedroom 'hung a picture that he had recently cut out of an illustrated magazine and housed in a nice, gilded frame. It showed a lady fitted out with a fur hat and fur boa who sat upright, raising a heavy fur muff that covered the whole of her lower arm towards the viewer.'

Schulz came to literature late and by chance. The name of that chance was Debora Vogel, his poet friend who lived in Lemberg. They had been writing each other long letters when, bedridden with illness, she suddenly begged Schulz to send her news from Drohobych. Rather than telling her about the weather or the local gossip, Schulz decided to write some fantastical stories to entertain her and, as Julien Gracq would say, 'to triumph over agony with the extraordinary'. Schulz looked at everything around him and metamorphosed it into fiction, particularly his father, Jacob, whom he transformed into a crab, a cockroach and a puppet, depending on the needs of his story. While Kafka depicted his father as an oppressive ogre, Schulz described his, in the story 'Cinnamon Shops', as a shrivelled little man, extremely sensitive to 'the unseen world of mouseholes, dark corners, chimney vents and dusty spaces under the floor'.

Vogel kept all the stories that he sent to her, and eventually convinced a publisher in Warsaw, Rój, to print two collections: *Cinnamon Shops*, in 1933, and *Sanatorium under the Sign of the Hourglass*, in 1937. Schulz didn't publish anything other than these two books. He wrote a short story in German, entitled 'The Homecoming' (1937), and allegedly sent it to Thomas Mann, but it was lost in the post. The manuscript of the novel that he worked on until his death, provisionally entitled *Messiah*, has also never been found.

Schulz's growing fame among literary circles in Warsaw during the 1930s did not change his daily life very much, but it did enable one thing: the translation of Kafka into Polish.

Let's rewind.

In 1932, Schulz met Józefina Szelińska, a young teacher from Drohobych, who became his fiancée between 1933 and 1937. Part of what fuelled their passion was the discovery of a mutual love of two writers from Prague: Franz Kafka – whom they both read in the original German in 1927[3] – and the poet Rainer Maria Rilke. Szelińska had even started translating *The Trial* into Polish, as a sort of hobby. She translated German books the way a musician might play scales: to train herself, without any illusions about her chances of being published. It would have seemed crazy, she thought, to approach publishers about such a proposal, given that she was just a provincial schoolteacher and

Kafka was still obscure. Only Schulz, whose name was now known in literary circles, would be able to persuade a publisher of the importance of such a project. He succeeded. Then he and Szelińska translated the book together. Once it was finished, Rój rushed to print it, accompanied with an afterword by Schulz. Although they shared the royalty payments equally, Józefina's name did not appear anywhere on that edition.[4]

In his afterword, Schulz put himself in Josef K's place: the only thing the poor man did wrong, he wrote, was to believe that he might emerge unscathed from his trial by 'clinging to his human reason'. In other words, Josef K was naive to imagine that the reign of stupidity would cease immediately when confronted with its opposite. Perhaps Josef K might have survived if, instead of questioning the judges about the legitimacy of the trial, instead of wearing himself out trying to make them see reason, he had simply obeyed their instructions. What Schulz proposed for Josef K was not the feigning of stupidity – he left that strategy to the hero of Jaroslav Hašek's *Good Soldier Švejk* – but docility. To act *as if* it all made sense. To pretend. To abase himself at the feet of his masters, as Schulz did in his drawings.

* * *

In 1941, Poland came under the control of the Third Reich: twelve thousand Jews – half the remaining population of Drohobych – were crammed into a ghetto. Schulz was one of them.

Nazism was obsessed with blood, which had to be purified, but also with soil – and in particular with gaining more of it. In practical terms, this expansion of the nation's *Lebensraum* translated into the installation of new residents in the houses left 'vacant' (that was the official term) by the Jews who had been kicked out of them. So it was that SS-Hauptscharführer Felix Landau could move into a villa that had previously belonged to the Jochmann family.

Renamed the 'Villa Landau', it became a show home. Not one of those empty shells used by estate agents to sell houses to buyers; they don't show much of anything. I'm talking about the kind of house whose walls bear witness to all that a century can inflict upon its occupants.

One monumental example of this is the Villa Tugendhat in Brno, the home town of Milan Kundera. Built by the Berlin architect Mies van der Rohe in 1929–30 at the request of a young, wealthy Jewish couple, the house would not be home (or at least not for very long) to the family for which it had been designed. The Tugendhats fled Czechoslovakia during the *Anschluss*, and their house was requisitioned by the Gestapo in 1939, then by the communist authorities in 1948. In 1992, it was used by the Czech and Slovak prime ministers to negotiate the two countries' separation, and after that the local government of Brno took it over. In 2001, the apogee of dispossession was reached when UNESCO named it a World Heritage site: now the house belonged to everyone, except to the people who, in 1929, had hoped to make it their *pokoj*. Located a few hundred yards from the house where Kundera was born, it's now in the control of the local mayor and open to the public. The initial layout of the rooms has been restored, and the original furniture reproduced. Entering it, you find yourself in 1930, when Herr and Frau Tugendhat had just moved in. Or perhaps in 1938, when they left it behind and ran for their lives.

I visited this villa one spring day. At the entrance, I was handed a pair of plastic slippers and a map of each room entitled *Mapa pokoju* – 'map of the *pokoj*'.

There are kidnapped countries, just as there are kidnapped villas. The *pokoj* is never safe from the threat of forced entry, as Kundera reminds us in his 1983 essay, 'A Kidnapped West'. All abductors, whether Soviet or Nazi, do the same thing: they erase the past. They want to make people forget that Prague, Brno or Drohobych once belonged to Western, democratic Europe. In 1938, this same Europe agreed to draw a vertical line through its centre, indicating the countries, west of that line, who deserved to be defended, and those in the East whom it could live without. In response, the kidnappers traced other lines, horizontal this time, to cross out methodically the entries in land registers, the registrations of births and deaths, the street names on signs, the words carved in pediments. The Villa Tugendhat, like the Villa Landau, was kidnapped in Kundera's sense of the word. The new owners didn't merely change the name on the letterbox; they transformed the entire civilisation from which the houses had emerged. These villas were no longer houses – they became display cases. Vivariums.

* * *

The Gestapo turned the secondary school in Drohobych into a sorting centre. Schulz, the art teacher, was summoned there to catalogue the artworks pillaged from the surrounding houses. Thousands of objects passed through his hands, including the libraries that the deported families could not take with them to the ghetto. (I am reminded of the Czech writer Bohumil Hrabal and his 1976 novel *Too Loud a Solitude*, in which the main character descends into madness after being sent to a cellar and forced to choose which books should be pulped and which spared.)

Felix Landau became aware of Schulz's artistic work, and one day he offered him a terrible bargain: Schulz could decorate the bedroom belonging to Landau's son in return for food. Essentially, he had to paint fairy tales with a revolver pressed to his temple, since he had neither the right nor the luxury of refusing. The deal meant that he had a safe-conduct pass allowing him to leave the ghetto so he could work at the villa. He turned up the next day with his paintbrushes. The longer he spent working on those friezes, the longer he was able to delay his deportation and to perfect his escape plan. You see, Josef K, this is what it means to feign docility.

Landau forced him to obey his most sadistic whims, far worse than the kind of things Schulz had imagined in his drawings. There was a German word for this role: *Leibjude*, or 'personal Jew'. Just because a Jew deserves death doesn't mean he can't be of service. Schulz was not the only Jew working at the Villa Landau, either. There were also nannies, servants and gardeners. Sometimes Landau would shoot at his staff without warning, just because he was in a bad mood. He even boasted about it. Like a forerunner of the antisemites of our own time, who proudly record their atrocities against Jews on GoPro cameras, Landau kept a daily logbook of his killings.[5]

On 19 November 1942, a few days before he could flee Drohobych with false papers, Schulz was shot in the back of the neck with two bullets on a street corner. Not by Landau, but by his SS rival, Karl Günther, who killed Schulz as revenge – Landau had killed 'his' *Leibjude*, a dentist who had been looking after Günther's teeth. One Jew each: Landau and Günther were now quits.

It is said that Schulz was secretly buried by a former student, Leopold Lustig, who recognised his corpse and carried it to the Jewish cemetery. This burial place no longer exists: it was destroyed after the war by the Russians, who erected a *khruschveka* – a five-storey apartment block – on the land it once occupied. History is not always manifested in a triumphant parade of tanks. Sometimes a single bulldozer, levelling a field of gravestones, is enough.

* * *

The Villa Landau was not restored to the Jochmann family after the war. (Were they still alive, even? Nobody knows.) The Soviet authorities, having taken over the country, requisitioned it and divided it into five apartments.

Around the same time, in 1947, Felix Landau – now operating under a false identity – took refuge in Stuttgart, Germany, where he started, with a disconcerting absence of irony, *an interior design agency for private customers.*

* * *

In 2001, ten years after Ukraine gained its independence, a father-and-son team of documentary makers from Hamburg, Benjamin and Christian Geissler, went in search of Schulz. Accompanied by Alfred Schreyer – a former student of Schulz also known as 'the last Jew in Drohobych' – the Geisslers turned up one morning, camera rolling, on the first floor of the Villa Formerly Known As Landau's, at 14 Tarnowski Street. A couple in their seventies, Mr and Mrs Kaluzhni, opened the door to them. Hello, the Geisslers said, we are looking for a certain Mr Schulz.

The filmmakers began searching every inch of the apartment, watched by the gaping Kaluzhnis. What were these Germans doing, scratching at their walls? And why were they moving towards the *Špajz*? Pronounced *shpaijz*, this is a sort of pantry, similar to the one that existed at my grandparents' apartment in Prague, a small room smelling of garlic, yeast and cabbage. The air there is somehow simultaneously fresh and suffocating. Each *Špajz* contains its very own cinnamon shop, at least in the sense that Schulz meant it in his story 'August': 'In that old familiar smell was contained a marvellously simple synthesis of the life of those people, the distillation of their race, the quality of their blood and the secret of their fate, imperceptibly mixed day by day with the passage of their own, private, time.'

And it is here, behind the jars of sweet-sour gherkins, in the pantry that contained 'the secret of their fate', that the documentary makers suddenly discovered the outlines of a princess, a dwarf, a flautist and a carriage. Schulz's pigments had managed to seep through all the different coats of paint that had been layered on top of them. In art terminology, as Benjamin Balint noted in his excellent biography of Bruno Schulz, this rebellion against oblivion has the evocative name of a *pentimento*, from the Italian verb *pentirsi*, meaning 'to repent'. To repent is to repair, and Schulz's *pentimento* called for numerous reparations. The Geisslers immediately informed the Polish, Ukrainian and Israeli authorities of their discovery. Who could have guessed that such news would trigger a diplomatic crisis? All three countries sent emissaries to Drohobych to examine the murals. The Kaluzhnis' apartment was subjected to all kinds of X-rays, ultraviolet and infrared lights. Rather than feeling as if they had been picked out for some unique destiny, the Kaluzhnis simply felt put out. 'They're not even paintings, just smears on the wall. It would be different if they were frescoes, Italian, Michelangelo or something,'[6] Mrs Kaluzhni told reporters. 'We knew about this house's past [...] but who could have imagined we'd never get any peace thanks to some old smears on the wall?'[7] Her husband, Nikolai, even threatened to knock down the damned walls with an axe if they weren't left in peace. Give me back my home, he begged. Give me my *pokoj* back: my room *and* my tranquillity.

After all, Mr and Mrs Kaluzhni had not asked for any of this. They had lived in that apartment for almost half a century, and now there was talk of them being evicted so that their home could be converted into a museum, and welcome tourists into their pantry. They felt like intruders in their own kitchen, in the company of murals that watched them and judged them. The walls had become the loudhailers of history. A short story by Schulz, entitled 'Mr Charles' (1933), describes very precisely the emotions of a man who suddenly feels he is being spied on by his own walls: 'the furniture and the walls watched him in silent criticism. [...] He felt, entering that stillness, like an intruder in an underwater kingdom with a different, separate notion of time. [...] Opening his own drawers, he felt like a thief and could not help moving on tiptoe, afraid to arouse noisy and excessive echoes that waited irritably for the chance to explode on the slightest provocation.'

It all came down to this question: to whom did Bruno Schulz belong? The Poles, the Ukrainians and the Israelis each had their own legitimate reasons to claim him. Poland venerated him as a national writer, Ukraine as a local boy, Israel as an integral part of the global Jewish heritage.

Is it really a fitting tribute to an artist to transform his prison into a monument? asked the emissaries from Jerusalem. Besides, how many tourists would even come here? Most people couldn't pinpoint Drohobych on a map, never mind pronounce it.

True, replied the Polish authorities, but Schulz never wrote a single line in Hebrew and only attended the synagogue once a year. Yet he was a pillar of the Polish literary avant-garde. Yes, let's talk about your synagogue, retorted the emissaries from Jerusalem. Have you seen it, the synagogue in Drohobych? A pathetic ruin with broken windows.[8] And even if Schulz never set foot there, he was still murdered solely because he was a Jew. All this is undeniable, agreed the Ukrainian authorities, but Schulz lived his whole life in Drohobych, so surely it would be barbarous to tear his work away from its roots and repot it fifteen hundred miles away. Let's be serious, responded the gentlemen from Jerusalem: the Drohobych that Schulz once knew no longer exists anywhere except in his prose. Schulz has no home or descendants or grave or archives in this town. There is nothing left to tie him to the land that was supposedly his, to the *pokoj* that once made his work possible. All that remains of him is a section of a wall that he painted with a gun to his head.

This debate, which could have gone on forever, was brought to an end on the night of 20–21 May 2001, when Israeli envoys prised the murals from the wall of the *Špajz* and chartered a jet to secretly transport them to Jerusalem, where they are now exhibited at the Yad Vashem memorial.[9] They are still there now. So it was that, after his death, Schulz made the escape that he wasn't able to make while he was alive.

'Operation Schulz' was, of course, carried out without informing the Ukrainian or Polish authorities, who instantly denounced it as an 'abduction'.[10] Mr and Mrs

K were blamed for having permitted – and even covered up – this exfiltration. How much money were they given? What were they promised in return for such a treasure? Nothing at all, they told reporters. It was just a *pokoj* barter. Jerusalem offered Schulz a new *pokoj*, and Mr and Mrs K got theirs back.

So what does all this have to do with Kafka?

Like Schulz's murals, Kafka's manuscripts were the object of a dispute between two institutions that claimed custody of them. The Deutsches Literaturarchiv in Marbach on one side, and the National Library of Israel in Jerusalem on the other. To whom did these manuscripts – rescued by Max Brod when he fled Prague in 1938 – belong? To the temple of Germanophone literature? Or to the state that, since 1948, has sought to represent all the world's Jews and, by extension, to collect their artefacts? Symbolically, there were three bodies in opposition: the body politic (Israel and Germany); the body of the text (a corpus written in German); and the writer's body (which rests in Prague).

The legal battle was fierce and went on for decades. It began as a basic succession dispute in a Tel Aviv family court, and ended up in the Israeli supreme court, which ruled in 2016 that the manuscripts should be sent to the National Library in Jerusalem. It is not insignificant that this battle started at a family court, presided over by judges who usually rule on divorce cases. The battle for Kafka, as with the battle for Schulz, marked a separation. Jewish culture had been happily married to Austrian–Slavic–Hungarian culture: for several centuries, the couple had lived under the same roof in a loving – if occasionally stormy – relationship producing many beautiful children, including Kafka and Schulz. But this household had been torn apart irrevocably in the mid-1930s. And this was followed by the usual loaded question: who would get custody of the kids? The argument grew all the more bitter since there was no possibility of shared custody. And all the more impassioned since it enabled the parents to make up for the relative indifference they had shown previously to their now-famous progeny.

What intellectual gymnastics must a nation perform to claim the inheritance of two writers who died before it even existed? In love as in law, at home as in international politics, notions of property and belonging are rarely unequivocal. In the twentieth century, they came into play whenever tribute was being paid to men and women who were reclaimed by more than one grateful country: at funeral services, or Nobel Prize awards ceremonies. Take, for example, the Nobel Prize in Literature won by the novelist Olga Tokarzcuk in 2018. Was she the eighteenth or the sixteenth Polish laureate? How should her compatriots Czesław Miłosz (1980) and Isaac Bashevis Singer (1978) be categorised, given that they received their prizes while exiled in the United States? The podium was disputed by the *ius solis* (right of the soil), the *ius sanguinis* (right of blood) and the *ius linguarum* (right of languages). The paths of these writers – to whom could be added Rainer Maria Rilke, Joseph Brodsky, Elsa Triolet, Vladimir Nabokov, Paul Celan and Witold Gombrowicz – all crossed at this point: they were claimed by everyone except their own homeland. Evicted from their apartments, exiled from their countries, stripped of their names, silenced in their mother tongues, these writers nonetheless (and often against their will) became the objects of what Pierre Nora called a 'realm of memory'. Like Schulz – who noted one day that he was 'a public employee, an Austrian, a Jew, a Pole – all in the space of an afternoon', – they belonged to more and more categories even as they transcended them.

Like an heir getting worked up in a solicitor's office, national authorities can employ the most outlandish justifications to claim filiation with a famous writer. Or, in the language of politics, a state can posthumously 'reterritorialise' a writer who was 'deterritorialised' during his lifetime. Think of Elias Canetti, whose Nobel Prize in 1981 was simultaneously claimed by seven different countries: Bulgaria (his birthplace), Spain (the birthplace of his native language), Germany (the birthplace of his written language), Turkey (the land of his old passport), Austria (where he wrote some of his books), England (the land of his new passport), and

Switzerland (where he had residency). Think, too, of the graveside brawl between representatives of France, Ukraine, Poland, Austria, the Catholics, the Jews, the communists and the monarchists over the novelist Joseph Roth in the Thiais cemetery, outside Paris, at his funeral in May 1939. Like Schulz, Roth was born in Galicia: he grew up in a village called Brody, not far from Drohobych. On the day of his funeral, each of those communities wanted to bury him in their own particular way. But no cross or Star of David would ever decorate his tomb. In 1970, the Austrian embassy laid a tombstone engraved with the simple inscription: 'Austrian writer'. And that was it. He couldn't possibly escape after that.

* * *

Should an artwork created by a people in exile follow the movements of that people? In other words, does a diaspora possess some sort of natural right to own any work of art created by one of its members? These questions are complicated by the fact that Schulz and Kafka so rarely ventured beyond the borders of their homelands. They also refused to define themselves by their belonging to or supposed filiation from any particular community. And, most perplexingly, what are we to make of the Kafka who, in January 1914, wrote in his diary: 'What do I have in common with

Jews? I have scarcely anything in common with myself?'

Israel, Poland, Ukraine: the nations fighting over Schulz, just like those fighting over Kafka's manuscripts, did everything they could to bask in the glow of these writers' haloes. But these are no ordinary nations. As I write this, all three are facing existential threats. They are what Kundera called 'small nations'. Not in terms of their surface area, but because history keeps reminding them that their existence, as Kundera wrote, 'may be put in question at any moment' by their neighbours. Every small nation knows that the treaties ratifying its borders are written on paper that could easily be turned into confetti. It knows that it must base its existence on something other than its topography or its physical borders. It needs a plan B, or some kind of life insurance. And this insurance is art – literature in particular – which becomes a potential ersatz territory. It enables the nation to legitimise through language what the hazards of geopolitics cannot guarantee: a *pokoj*, whose existence is all the more necessary since the nation's borders are fragile.

Emmanuel Levinas, a Lithuanian Jewish philosopher who migrated to France, put it most succinctly: 'Attachment to cultural forms appears to be the same thing as attachment to the land.' In this way, the small nation tells the world that it did not appear out of nowhere, but that it is the continuation of a lineage. The lives and works of Schulz and Kafka preceded the official births of Poland, Ukraine and Israel: proof, if proof were needed, that these nations, however small, deserved to exist.

KAFKA AND HEBREW

THE PROMISED TRANSLATION

What is Hebrew, if not news from afar?

Kafka, letter to Robert Klopstock (1923)

Kafka's work was translated into Hebrew only belatedly, in a piecemeal fashion, and the first published versions were not received with any great enthusiasm. Such faint-heartedness seems surprising. The translation into Hebrew of a work created at the crossroads of two worlds – the Jewish and the Germanic – ought to have been eagerly awaited. It was not.

Translation naturally requires the existence of at least two languages. But this much-needed translation of Kafka coincided with a historical moment when the viability of both German and Hebrew were being called into question. Could Hebrew really become something more than a biblical language? Could German ever again be anything other than the idiom of death?

* * *

On 6 September 1913, Kafka left Prague on a business trip to Vienna. His employer, the Workers' Accident Insurance Institute for the Kingdom of Bohemia, had dispatched him to a very serious conference on accident prevention. As chance would have it, in that same city of Vienna, on that same day, the eleventh World Zionist Congress came to town. The Archduke Franz Ferdinand had not yet been assassinated, but Vienna was already attracting the anxious: insurers on one side, Zionists on the other. Two separate conference rooms for two shared concerns: self-protection and damage control.

First organised by the Viennese activist Theodor Herzl in 1897, the World Zionist Congress was held every two years, often in a different city. Even though Kafka had kept a safe distance from all political movements, he found it impossible to ignore the event. His curiosity won out over his terror of crowds, and he took his place in the audience of six hundred. Among them he saw 'Palästinafahrer', as he mockingly called central European Jews who journeyed to the Holy Land with a little too much messianic zeal for his liking.[1] He viewed them as we might view a friend who quits his job to join a Nepalese ashram, citing vague spiritual ideals.

Kafka was accompanied by his childhood friend Hugo Bergmann, a philosopher and librarian at the University of Prague. Kafka could not know this, but Bergmann would, a few years later, become director of the National

Library of Jerusalem: the same institution that would, almost a century after that, declare Kafka 'a national treasure' and claim custody of his manuscripts.

Next to them was a young Galician novelist by the name of Shmuel Yosef Agnon, who would, in 1966, become the first (and, so far, the only) Hebrew-language writer to win the Nobel Prize in Literature.

A few rows away sat a certain Salman Schocken, a businessman from Berlin who would later publish this same Agnon, as well as the complete works of Kafka in German, English and Hebrew.

Several feet further on were Chaim Weizmann, a chemist of Belarusian origin who was teaching at the University of Manchester, and, beside him, a certain David Grün, who would later be better known under the name of David Ben-Gurion. In 1948, these two men would become, respectively, the first president and the first prime minister of a state that, back in 1913, existed only in their heads.

Quite the crowd, then, but none of them – and none of the speeches given during the congress – impressed Kafka. The whole Zionist project struck him as dubious, and about as viable as a house of cards. He summarised his impressions in three lines of a letter sent to his fiancée at the time, Felice Bauer: 'The delegates from Palestine yelled constantly'; 'Herzl's daughter was present; the speeches were useless and depressing'. The event, in short, struck him as 'totally alien'. He wrote to

Max Brod with the heavy heart of a man who regretted a wasted day: 'It is hard to imagine anything more useless than such a congress.' He was baffled by the audience's apparent fascination with Jerusalem. Why were they so obsessed with that dusty old city? Various religious and ethnic communities shared the same space without interacting, and they dared to call that a new start? He might as well stay in Prague, it was the same story there.

The company of Goethe and Schiller, and the dream of joining the highest spheres of the German literary canon, inspired Kafka far more than the company of the people at the Zionist Congress. His promised land, or at least the land he promised himself he would one day reach, was called Weimar.

* * *

Whether it was held in Vienna, Czernowitz, Prague, Basel or Vilnius, every Zionist gathering rekindled the same debate: which language would they speak in the Promised Land? Hebrew? Yiddish? Arabic? German?[2] They needed a language that could both unite the immense diaspora and make it exist in the eyes of the world. An insider language that would be recognised by the outside world. But how could they choose only one? The political demands of the Czechs, Hungarians, Poles,

Ukrainians and Romanians that were shaking the Russian and Austro-Hungarian Empires seemed far less complicated: to become masters of their destinies, these national minorities could each unite around their common language as a first step to territorial independence. The Jewish minorities, scattered all over the world, came up against the opposite problem. Their 'nation' was projected to exist within precise borders, but not within a precise language. For how many centuries had the diaspora repeated the phrase 'next year in Jerusalem'? Would the biblical canon and its alphabet be enough to make that dream a reality?

Linguistically, as in so many other ways, Zionism was a giant melting pot of contradictory tendencies. Would it mean a break with tradition or a continuation? Every answer to the question had a different vision, expressed in a different language. Those opposed to Yiddish argued that it was not actually a language, merely a jargon composed of root words clumped together. Alfred Polgar, a Jewish journalist from Vienna, compared Yiddish to unleavened bread. It was the sound of a people that had been hunted a thousand times over. This language carried within it the absence of a *pokoj*, the lack of a private space and a sense of peace. The critics of Yiddish believed that the language of the ghetto would keep its speakers confined to the ghetto, incapable of escape.

Those opposed to Hebrew, on the other hand, pointed out that nobody had spoken this language since the destruction of the Second Temple in 70 CE – not in the streets, the sheets, nor the cradle. Hebrew continued to exist only as the language of the Bible and the synagogue's rites. And it was not a *pokoj* language any more than Yiddish was. Above all, you couldn't use a sacred language for everyday life without risking God's wrath. Surely it was profanity to speak the language of God to buy a pair of socks? The arguments provoked by this question were all the thornier since another problem had arisen: if Jews limited themselves to the lexicon of the Bible, they ran the risk of causing a retreat into religious isolationism, in direct opposition to the promised emancipation of a Zionism that claimed to be inspired by Enlightenment ideals. How could they build a modern nation without the words for electricity, aeroplanes, rockets? Therein lay the difficulty: a secular movement employing the language of worship.

Then again, if you swept away the foundations of Hebrew with a wave of neologisms, there was a danger that you would render it meaningless. Stripped of its ancestral quality, what could it offer a young nation? These questions plunged the most pious thinkers into a state of quasi-apocalyptic despair. For a kabbalist, every letter of the alphabet contains a fragment of the divine, and every word possesses a hidden meaning. Reworking the language's structures would upset the equilibrium of the world and scramble the frequencies through which the Word of God was made audible.[3] This anxiety was particularly palpable in the writings of Gershom Scholem. A Zionist and Hebrew scholar, he was vehemently opposed to the modernisation of the sacred language, fearful that it would provoke a divine vengeance. In 1926, three years after moving to Jerusalem, and long before the proclamation of the State of Israel, he warned: 'What will be the result of updating the Hebrew language? Is not the holy language, which we have planted among our children, an abyss that must open up? [...] One day the language will turn against its own speakers [...]. Will we then have a youth who will be able to hold fast against the rebellion of a holy tongue?'

To summarise: Yiddish was very popular, but not sacred enough; Hebrew was too sacred, but not popular enough. The challenge was to invent a nation that could welcome both those who considered kabbalistic dialectics to be essential and those who couldn't care less about them. The discussions did not go well. Kafka was no kabbalist, but he was tormented by the opacity of language, or rather its inadequacy. In 1920, he rewrote the myth of the Tower of Babel as a brief parable entitled 'The City Coat of Arms'.[4] The reason the Tower of Babel remained as nothing more than a sketch, the narrator claims, is not because of some divine punishment, but because several generations of builders failed to agree on the paperwork and the choice of materials to construct it. Likewise, every Zionist Congress replayed the same controversy: in what language should the building permit be written?

* * *

Theodor Herzl, the founder and apostle of the Zionist movement, did not imagine for a second that Yiddish or Hebrew could become the language of a modern state. His vision of Zionism was not preoccupied with metaphysics or linguistics, but with history. The return of the Jews mattered more to him than the return of the Messiah. So he did not see it as a problem that each new arrival in Palestine should bring his own language with him. The Jews would manage there as they managed everywhere else: by being multilingual. Don't forget that his manifesto, written in 1896, just before the first Zionist Congress in Basel, was entitled *Der Judenstaat – The Jewish State* (or, as some translators have rendered it, *The Jews' State*), not *The Hebrew State*. 'Someone may think that difficulties will arise from the fact that we no longer share a common language. After all, we cannot converse with one another in Hebrew. Who among us knows enough Hebrew to ask for a railroad ticket in that language? We have no such people. Yet it is really a very simple matter. Everyone will retain his own language, the beloved homeland of his thoughts. Switzerland offers conclusive proof that linguistic federalism is possible.'

'The beloved homeland of his thoughts': isn't this a beautiful definition of the *pokoj*? You could take Herzl out of Vienna, but you couldn't take Vienna out of Herzl. It was too deeply embedded. His ideal of the state was shaped by Austro-Hungarian culture, and the multilingual coexistence he had experienced there. Vienna tolerated multiple identities. Why not simply teleport that system to Jerusalem? To each according to his *pokoj* and to each according to his needs: a place for Jews wearing top hats as much for those Jews wearing fur hats. German would be the language of government, universities and the press, as it was in Vienna. And if you passed a *Herr Professor Doktor* on the street, as you did on the Ringstrasse, you would greet him respectfully. In other words, Herzl dreamed of a Middle Eastern Vienna, albeit with fewer antisemites.

Because it was written for the Basel congress, Herzl's manifesto advocated the example of Switzerland's 'linguistic federalism'. No doubt this system struck him as more consensual, or more neutral, than the Austro-Hungarian microcosm. Fifteen years later, in the summer of 1911, Kafka went to Switzerland on one of his first journeys outside Prague. Together with Max Brod, he recorded his impressions in a spiral notebook, interspersed with doodles and exchange rate calculations. (The Austro-Hungarian crown was shrinking in the shadow of the Swiss franc.) When they got to Zurich, Kafka and Brod were surprised to see signs in a bathhouse written in French, German, English and Italian.[5] They naturally drew a parallel with Prague, where linguistic quarrels between Czechs and Germans were growing ever louder. 'The Swiss think they can settle the linguistic question with signs,' they observed. Then they changed their minds: these signs did not bring order to the linguistic chaos, they simply made it official.

Certain speed limits were expressed in French but not in Italian, while certain turns, permitted in German, were forbidden in French. And so on. It became impossible – even for someone of good faith – to travel a hundred yards without breaking some kind of law. The Swiss legal system made sense only to the person who understood its meaning – nobody, in other words – and, as in a Kafka story, it only emerged to issue fines. In this sense, Switzerland was a truly Kafkaesque land: there, ignorance of the law constituted proof of guilt. Brod and Kafka concluded that, in a multilingual country, people could get used to the coexistence of multiple languages only on the condition that they could get used to the nonexistence of meaning. This system made Switzerland 'certainly a school for statesmen', wrote Kafka in his notebook, quoting Brod. Presumably they would have smiled if they could have seen the United Nations establish its headquarters there thirty-five years later.

* * *

Whether it was debated in Hebrew, Yiddish, German or some multilingual combination, the Zionist project brought Kafka no consolation. Not that he couldn't speak these languages: he was fluent in German and Czech, could understand Yiddish, and – from 1917 on – studied Hebrew so conscientiously that he was able to carry on a sustained correspondence with his teacher. But that did not stop Kafka suffering the same fate as all polyglots: not feeling at home in any of the languages he spoke.

He articulated the problem in a letter to Max Brod in June 1921: 'For a Jew, writing in German is like appropriating a foreign property that does not belong to you, and it remains foreign even if you do not make the slightest linguistic error.' There was always someone to remind him that his love for the German language was not reciprocated. Or to detect some trace of foreignness, as if there existed a wall that no amount of knowledge could ever knock down. He went on: 'I use this language because I don't have another one, but it isn't mine.' He might just as easily have rewritten that sentence, replacing the word 'language' with 'people' or 'land'. None of these terms were self-evident. And yet there was nothing unusual about Kafka in this sense. 'I am a typical western Jew,' he explained to Milena in November 1920. 'In other words, I am not granted a second's peace.' No peace, and no *pokoj*. No language could alleviate the absence of a homeland, nor could it offer a space where he might put down roots. The Zionist project offered a glimpse of a place he could call his own, but no hint of a language he might speak there.

* * *

In 1948, when the State of Israel was proclaimed, Ben-Gurion declared: 'One language, one people.' The language would be Hebrew, which 'alone' could provide Jews with the anchor that had been stolen from them two thousand years before. After years of wandering, they would have a homeland at last. As the Russian-born philosopher Isaiah Berlin said ironically: 'The Jewish people? We have rather too much history, and too little geography.' The Hebrew language would connect their history and their geography, like a house being connected to the electrical grid. Suddenly the lights would come on and the Jews would be able to move around without bumping into things.

* * *

The first translation of Kafka into Hebrew was made at the behest of the publisher and businessman Salman Schocken who – between 1935 and 1937, at the height of Nazism – had somehow contrived to publish the complete works of Kafka in German. In 1938, when his Berlin-based publishing house had been banned, he moved it to Tel Aviv. The Hebrew translation was his way of fertilising this new land: he 'planted' literature there as other settlers planted orange trees. He fed the Hebrew language on foreign masterpieces the way he might have given his own child vitamins to help them grow. For Shmuel Agnon, a translator was a builder; each new translation built upon the previous one: 'Hebrew was not yet in a position to supply one word for another. Anyone who translated into Hebrew was taking part in the construction of the Hebrew language. We would study a word together and discuss its meaning day and night, struggling with concepts that are so simple and easy in another language, and yet so difficult and incomprehensible in Hebrew.' The strength and solidity of Hebrew would be measured by the strength and solidity of the literary works that were brought to life within it. This flood of translations was accompanied, in 1953, by the foundation of the Academy of the Hebrew Language.[6] Its mission was in some ways the opposite of what the Académie Française does now: rather than policing neologisms, it produced them.

The language was constructed as if it were a house. Step one: dig the foundations. The Hebrew translator had to excavate meanings like an archaeologist, as illustrated by Martin Buber in the pages of his magazine *Der Jude*: 'Through its contents, [Hebrew] passes on to us essential, lost values, and in its form it resurrects Jewish thought patterns that have been suppressed or silenced by European languages or other mother tongues.'

Reading Kafka in Hebrew illuminated elements of the work that had been buried by the German language.

Amerika, translated by the writer Yitzhak Shenhar, was the first Kafka novel to appear in Hebrew, in 1945. Since it's the story of the misadventures of a young migrant arriving in New York without a suitcase or papers or any idea where to go, Schocken was perhaps hoping that readers recently arrived at the port of Jaffa would recognise themselves in the main character. But the translation was met with general indifference.

In 1951, Schocken tried again, commissioning the writer Yeshurun Keshet to translate *The Trial*. However, Schocken's friend Gershom Scholem, having obtained a preview copy, thought it was so bad that he begged Schocken – in the name of their shared admiration for Kafka – not to publish it.[7] And that was that. Schocken died in 1959, without another Kafka translation being published in Israel.

Why such disinterest, when Kafka's work was becoming famous all over the world? Partly because, in the postwar years, Hebrew was the native language of almost nobody. It is also perhaps true that the ongoing modernisation of Hebrew didn't make it especially easy to publish or translate in that language. But it is reasonable to think that these are not the only explanations.

In the wake of the war, the language of Goethe and Kafka became as undesirable in Israel as Dostoevsky's mother tongue is now in Ukraine. The memory of that language was widespread, but nowhere was it praised. In this country where a third of the inhabitants were Holocaust survivors, there was a boycott – albeit informal – of all things German. Having died before the publication of *Mein Kampf*, however, Kafka had taken no part in the transformations inflicted on the German language by the Nazis. He wasn't even German. So what was he being blamed for? Nothing, except the fact of having lived and written in a language that could no longer be considered harmless, if it ever had been. The language in which Auschwitz had been conceived was now so soiled that no translation, not even into Hebrew, could ever wash it clean. Not only that, but all the Jewish Germans and Austrians who had survived the Holocaust now felt a deep sense of shame at having contributed – through the *Bildung*: the arts and the sciences – to the spread of this language that had sentenced their loved ones to death.

* * *

Adolf Eichmann's trial in Jerusalem, from April to December 1961, loudly brought the German language back into the public sphere in Israel. The shock it caused was first and foremost acoustic: Israeli public radio broadcast almost every single hearing. The language of this zealous architect of the 'final solution of the Jewish problem' for the Third Reich was suddenly audible in people's homes, in shops and cafés, in factories and on buses.

Inside the courtroom, the shock was primarily visual. On the first day, a thin man, seeming too frail for the enormity of his crime, took his place behind armoured glass, a pair of headphones covering his ears. Those headphones, connected to the banks of interpreters, came to represent the single most important *object* in the trial: language. It was through those headphones that the language of the people in whose name justice would be served – Hebrew – encountered the language of the man who had resolved to send that same people to their extermination – German.

The trial featured a system of simultaneous translation mocked by Hannah Arendt, there to report on the event for the *New Yorker*. Arendt tried plugging her own headphones into the different translation channels to follow the exchanges, and was surprised by the poor quality of the interpreters who were translating the judges' Hebrew and Eichmann's German. Wasn't there a single competent translator in this damn country? What she presumably didn't know – or perhaps pretended not to know – was that German was no longer taught in any Israeli school or university and that, among the people who had arrived from Germany fifteen years earlier, very few of them had an in-depth knowledge of Hebrew legalese. Not only that, but none of the interpreters had been prepared, linguistically or emotionally, to translate 'things no human mouth should ever have said'.[8] The silences and stammerings could not all be put down to ignorance of the language. They arose from the shock of being confronted with the reality of the Holocaust. What the interpreters were experiencing was incommunicability in its most radical form. This was not word-for-word translation but hand-to-hand combat. Several of the witnesses fainted while describing what they went through. Their legs gave way as their words dried up. And the same thing was happening behind the scenes: the interpreters sometimes had to turn off their microphones while they stifled their sobs.

* * *

The mistakes and delays in the translation process that annoyed Arendt were welcomed by Eichmann: every minute that passed between his responses and their laborious translation gave him time to prepare his next answer carefully. Joseph Kessel, covering the hearings for the newspaper *France Soir*, also grew irritated: the interpreters' hesitations slowed down what he called the 'sparring' between the judges and the accused. 'The shock of the revelations was lost. The prosecutor had to regain momentum from scratch every time.' Why did the judges put up with such a complicated linguistic process? For all three of them – Moshe Landau, Benjamin

Halevy and Yitzhak Raveh – German was their native language. They had all grown up in the Weimar Republic, whose liberal constitution had been written by a Jewish lawyer, Hugo Preuss, from the same social background. Brought up on the *Bildung* from nursery school to law school, they belonged to the same Jewish-German bourgeoisie as Kafka and his parents, a class that believed absolutely in assimilation and the promises of modernity. These three judges fled to Palestine in 1933, after the Nazi government banned them from teaching or practising law in Germany. So Eichmann was the principal reason for their presence in the courtroom: not only because they were his judges and he was the accused, but also because they had, by chance, escaped the fate to which this man believed he had condemned them.

The three judges were from Arendt's world too, and she in turn judged them to be one of the trial's saving graces. To her friend Karl Jaspers, she lauded the qualities of the 'modest, intelligent, very open' Judge Landau, who embodied what Arendt considered the 'best of German Jewry'. He was her kind of German Jew, in other words. She sensed a resonance between what had been her *pokoj* and the judges' own.

The seventh of July 1961 marked a turning point in the trial. That day, exasperated by the game Eichmann was playing during the cross-examination, the judges took off their headphones, cutting out the interpreters who had, until this point, provided a bridge of communication between prosecution and defence. The judges addressed Eichmann directly in German, breaking the rule that the trial should be conducted entirely in Hebrew. '[The prosecutor] no longer waited for Eichmann's words to be translated, nor for his own attack to be blunted or dampened by the interpreter's voice,' reported Kessel. The men came to German as other men might come to blows. Their questions arrived like punches to the face, impossible to dodge. Eichmann in turn took off his headphones too. Had he heard correctly? Having been completely unmoved by the testimonies of a hundred and eleven Holocaust survivors, he seemed utterly shocked by the sound of his own language coming from the judges' mouths. In switching to German, the judges were telling him that there still remained a patch of territory, a little *pokoj* where Germanness and Jewishness continued to overlap. By speaking German in that Israeli courtroom, they abruptly split that language between the two extremes of its own past.

The video recording of the trial shows the judges taking off their glasses just before they start speaking German. For 'glasses', read 'gloves'. The German language had been weaponised against them, against all Jews, but now they were turning that weapon back on its maker.

By expressing themselves in German, the judges reminded the audience that this language had not always been the preserve of the Nazis. They let people hear that 'other' German, from before 1933. They established a distinction between the language of the crime and their own language. These judges were not exclusively Jewish nor exclusively German: their *pokoj* was woven from both worlds, and they would not let it be torn apart.

This linguistic turnaround was crucial in two respects. First, for the rest of the trial, because it was in German that Eichmann's judges would pressure him into several confessions. And second, for the future of Kafka's work in Hebrew.

Was it necessary for Eichmann to go on trial in Israel before Kafka could be translated there? This might seem a dubious idea, but the chronology supports it. And it doesn't really matter that much whether it was the result of chance, causality or some unconscious machination. Let us simply note that three different Hebrew translations of Kafka were published in the aftermath of the Eichmann trial, and without one particular publisher behind the phenomenon. *The Castle* was published for the first time in 1967, *Letters to Milena* in 1976, and the *Diaries* in 1978.

The inversion of languages during Eichmann's trial also inverted, momentarily and symbolically, the balance of power within Kafka's *Trial*. Suddenly, German ceased to be the language of the defence and became the language of the accusation. It was no longer being used to clear the name of a criminal, but to pronounce his sentence.

Josef K was finally granted the wish that had been denied him in the novel: he was allowed to speak. And to judge his executioners.

KAFKA AND MILENA JESENSKÁ

A LOVE OF TRANSLATION

Languages are imperfect in that, although there are many, the supreme one is lacking: to think is to write without accessories, without whispering, but since the immortal word is still tacit, the diversity of tongues on Earth keeps everyone from uttering the words that would otherwise, in a single stroke, embody the material truth.

Stéphane Mallarmé, 'Crisis in Verse' (1897)

The first and only translator of his work that Kafka ever met was a woman. For a long time, she was known only by her first name, which in Czech means 'lover' or 'beloved': Milena. She was the recipient of the feverish and anxious letters that Kafka wrote between 1920 and 1923. Their correspondence, an intertwining of Czech and German, reads like a sustained, two-headed reflection on their two passions: for each other and for translation, as if they were two sides of the same coin. The words 'seduction' and 'translation' have this in common: they describe both a process (the act of seducing, the act of translating) and the result of that process (the transformed heart, the translated text). Above all, these letters seem to animate the theories of the German philosopher Walter Benjamin, articulated, albeit somewhat nebulously, in his short treatise 'The Task of the Translator', published in 1923: 'It is the task of the translator to release in his own language that pure language which is exiled among alien tongues, to liberate the language imprisoned in a work in his re-creation of that work.' One must read the letters to understand the lengths to which Milena went in her attempts to liberate Kafka from the torments that made him both an exile and a prisoner of Prague, his family, his illness, his 'burrow'.

For Walter Benjamin, languages are like souls: they roam ceaselessly in search of the one that will complete them. Written during the same years as the Franz–Milena correspondence, his essay sets the conditions for the possibility of an *encounter*. Taken individually, every language is semi-mute, or semi-extinct. The original and its translation become two fragments of the same broken vessel, he explains. Once they are glued together, they do not merely restore the vessel, but form 'a greater language' or 'a pure language'. Is that the meaning of the (admittedly abstruse) quotation by the French symbolist poet Mallarmé that I used as the epigraph to this chapter? Let's deconstruct it.

Languages are imperfect in that, although there are many, the supreme one is lacking ...: languages can complete and perfect themselves only by uniting with others. The ultimate aim of translation is to achieve this 'supreme' (or 'pure', in Benjamin's formulation) state, in which the two languages exist in such a way that notions of the original and the translation, of the familiar and the foreign, no longer mean anything. The wording of the work would be 'pure' and 'supreme' in that no single language could capture its totality. Rather than Benjamin's image of the broken vase, picture a mirrorball, where every language is a different reflective facet. One single facet, hanging pitifully from the ceiling on its own, would not be able to light up a nightclub, any more than a broken vessel could be used to pour drinks. But put them together and everything changes. The mirrorball reflects and scatters the light that it receives, just like languages reflecting the work that is projected onto them.

… *to think is to write without accessories, without whispering, but since the immortal word is still tacit* …: or, put more simply, thought is formed before being converted into words and languages. It does not need any accessory – any expression, written or oral. The same is true for the work: it's whole only as the sum of its translations, each one illuminating a previously unknown aspect. The work – the true, 'supreme' work – thus exists beyond languages, because it contains them all. It is like the negative of a film that must be dipped in multiple chemical baths to reveal all its nuances, all its colours, all the details hidden in the same photograph.

... the diversity of tongues on Earth keeps everyone from uttering the words that would otherwise, in a single stroke, embody the material truth: how can a language faithfully express a thought that was formulated without it? It's doomed to either betrayal or approximation. The same goes for translation: by transposing the work from a 'pure' or 'supreme' state into a vernacular state, from impenetrable to accessible, translation offers us only one aspect, the sparkle of a single facet, a half-truth.

The more translations of a work there are, the more the languages are superimposed. Benjamin writes of the 'hallowed growth of languages'. What we can understand by this is that translation is a red carpet leading to the supreme state. Or rather a staircase. The French playwright Sacha Guitry said that the best moment in love is the moment when you are climbing the stairs, and this is also true for the translator: she works her way from one translation to another up the steps that lead to perfection – to the summit of the Tower of Babel. To translate is to move closer to the original language in which Adam and Eve spoke under the apple tree.

* * *

Kafka's diary entry for 4 May 1915 seems simultaneously to foreshadow his meeting with Milena and anticipate Benjamin's eschatological ideas: 'There is no one here who understands me in my entirety. To have someone possessed of such understanding, a wife perhaps, would mean to have support from every side, to have God.' Unlike Kafka's unfortunate fiancées, Felice Bauer and Julie Wohryzek, who were neither seduced nor convinced by their lover's prose, Milena embraced the irreducible strangeness of Kafka.

* * *

Benjamin refutes the idea that the translator is a linguistic tourist in search of the exotic. Translation is not a travel agency. In fact, it's more like a dating agency: the source language and the target language do not know each other until a literary work gives them the opportunity to meet. A language is like Sleeping Beauty, waiting for the translator's kiss to awaken what always lay silent within. Translation *discovers*: it removes clothing and explores unknown lands. It is the meeting of Fragonard and Marco Polo, the intimacy of the boudoir and the expanse of the ocean.

Or, in Benjamin-speak, translation 'ultimately serves the purpose of expressing the innermost relationship of languages'. The translation neither eclipses nor duplicates the original: it strips it naked. It silently demolishes the border separating the original text from its foreign version. The inherent intimacy of translation is not to do with resemblance, but with secrets: the more the languages are connected by translation, the more they reveal their hidden meanings. Paul Valéry put it best: 'In the loving embrace of translation, languages – like lovers – open themselves to what they do not know.'[1]

Where Mallarmé and Benjamin dreamed of a world beyond words, Valéry perceived an immense risk: 'If language was perfect, man would cease to think.'[2] In other words, a perfect language, born from the intertwining of all the others, would eliminate not only thought, but love too. Translations and love letters are fuelled by the same ingredient: frustrated desire. You are not here, so I am writing to you. The right word isn't at the tip of my tongue, so I am seeking it at the tip of yours. The letter is aimed at the absent lover; translation is aimed at a language that is not its own. Both are powered by the impossibility of grasping what they lack in the other.

* * *

Milena and Kafka first met in Prague in the autumn of 1919 beneath the chandeliers of the Café Arco, a rallying point for the city's Jewish-German writers.[3] There, the daily newspaper was presented in a wooden frame, and coffee was served on a silver salver. Neither of them were regulars; Kafka had been dragged there that night by his friend Max Brod, and Milena by her husband, the

Austrian writer Ernst Pollak. Before that moment, Kafka had never imagined that his writings might interest the Czech literati, never mind such a young, attractive woman. He was probably a little wary, like Groucho Marx, of joining any club that would have him for a member, and incapable of opening himself to a woman who was interested in him.

* * *

Kafka was thirty-six, Milena was twenty-three. She wasn't Jewish; she came from a rigidly bourgeois and loudly antisemitic family. They both had passports in the name of the Czechoslovak Republic that had come into existence one year before. They each lived in isolation in a city that they hated. 'We are both married, you in Vienna, me to my fear in Prague,' he wrote to her. She was a Czech living in Vienna, while he was a German-speaking Jew living in Prague. Their chance meeting, although brief, changed both of their lives, precipitating Milena's divorce and Kafka's entry into the Czech literary world. In a letter dated 13 June 1920, he told her that she had 'come roaring' into his room like a 'storm'.

* * *

The night that they first met, Milena asked Kafka for permission to translate him into Czech for a small, avant-garde Czech magazine called *Kmen*.[4] He agreed, and Milena immediately set to work on translating the short story 'Der Heizer' (translated as 'The Stoker' in English – and 'Topič' in Czech). Kafka, who had only ever lived and worked in Prague, naturally knew the Czech language and Czech customs, but he was a nonentity in the eyes of this community, despite his proximity. 'I have never lived among the German people,' he wrote to Milena. 'German is my native language, so it feels natural to me, but Czech is closer to my heart, which means that your letter has dispelled much of my uncertainty: I see you more distinctly, the movements of your body, your hands, so quick, so decisive, it's almost like being with you.'

Although all of Milena's letters have disappeared – destroyed either by Kafka himself or by Wehrmacht troops when they entered Prague in 1939 – we can guess what she must have written. Given his legal training, it is perhaps no surprise that Kafka acted like the court clerk of their relationship. His letters all begin methodically with sentences such as 'You wrote in your last letter to me that …' or 'You state that …' or 'You ask me if …' or 'You mention that …', before responding point by point. Their correspondence was self-consciously sober and professional at first, but little by little their deeper feelings seeped between the lines: 'Dear Frau Milena' became 'Dear Milena', then the diminutive 'Milenka', then simply 'you'. The formal 'you' (*Sie*) became the informal 'you' (*du*), before metamorphosing into 'we' (*wir*). She sent him handwritten drafts as her translations progressed. Kafka would comment on them, annotate them, kiss them. In this relationship, where the miles between them were travelled more often in words than caresses, the act of unsealing an envelope was equivalent to unbuttoning a blouse, and holding one of her letters was like stroking her hips. 'Please send me your translation – I can't have enough of you in my hands.'[5]

* * *

Milena asked him one day if he would prefer her to write to him in Czech or in German. Like her, Kafka was fluent in both languages, so which should they choose? This was simply the linguistic version of a choice that all lovers face at some point: 'Your place or mine?'

He chose her place. 'I understand Czech, of course. I have wanted to ask you several times already why you weren't writing to me in Czech. Obviously I am not saying this because there is anything wrong with your German. [...] But I wanted to read you in Czech, because you belong to it – it is only really there that the whole Milena can be found, whereas here there is only the Milena from Vienna or the one who's getting ready for Vienna. So in Czech, please.' From that point on, it seemed that Milena wrote to him in Czech and that Kafka replied to her in German. Milena's translations sent from Vienna and Kafka's annotations sent from Prague marked a parallel correspondence that, to quote Benjamin again, helped 'ripen the seed of pure language'.

In Prague, Kafka would hear Czech all the time – on every street corner and in the office where he worked – but until his meeting with Milena, nobody had ever spoken to him so intimately with it. In 1920, only sixteen months after the proclamation of the Czechoslovak Republic, Czech became the official language and German a *lingua non grata*.[6] In a Europe undergoing the painful contractions of nationalism, more than a decade before the monstrous child of that labour would be born, the linguistic border acted as a line along which the territorial border could be traced. The continued existence of a German-speaking minority – and a Jewish minority, to boot – was a fly in the Czech soup. It provided an obstacle to the young nation's dreams of homogeneity. The two strains of nationalism – Czech on one side, and German on the other – turned out to be equally antisemitic. It was the clash of two forms of purism.

In a passage from *The Castle*, the protagonist, K the land surveyor, hears a new language coming through the telephone receiver: 'It was as if the murmur of countless childish voices [...] were forming, unlikely as that might be, into a single high, strong voice, striking the ear as if trying to penetrate further than into the mere human sense of hearing.' This image illustrates the situation of German-speaking Jews in 1920s Prague: having guessed that they would soon be driven away by this new language, many of them left Prague for Leipzig, Berlin, Vienna, Paris or Jerusalem. The ones who remained, like Kafka and Brod, found themselves doubly isolated – as Jews, and as German language speakers.

* * *

The future of Kafka's relationship with Milena was inextricably linked to the future of their respective countries. 'When you talk about the future don't you sometimes forget that I'm a Jew?'[7] Jewish German-speaking Czechs like Kafka belonged to a generation who had no homeland and did not believe in a promised land. Born in 1883, Kafka grew up in a Prague torn by disputes over identity, with the coexistence of Judaism, German and Czech – which his parents' generation had taken for granted – no longer guaranteed. The idea of multiple loyalties had come to seem suspect.

This anomaly obliged Kafka continually to justify his

existence, to initiate, almost pre-emptively, the trials that he imagined the people around him dreamed of inflicting on him.

Let's rewind again.

Thanks to Emperor Franz Joseph, who granted the Jews citizenship in 1867, Kafka's ancestors had benefited from a slow but fourfold migration: from eastern Bohemia to the capital; from the peasantry to the ranks of urban shopkeepers and the bourgeoisie; from orthodoxy to secular assimilation; and from Czech and Yiddish to German. The language in which their emancipation had been decreed was, for them, synonymous with social dignity. So it was that Kafka's parents had named him after that beneficent emperor – Franz.

Kafka's parents had managed to make a place for themselves in society. The same was not true for their son, whose generation witnessed the rise of antisemitism without understanding what they were supposed to have done. He had a solid legal status in Czechoslovakia, but felt like a foreigner there nonetheless. To Milena, he expressed the 'repugnant shame' he felt at 'living under protection' and wondered what the outside world, which he could see and hear from his window, could have against a man like him. He didn't have a skullcap or a beard or a kaftan, and he never attended the synagogue. What made him a Jew, exactly? His 'difference' seemed all the more disturbing because it was invisible. His generation were unprepared for the antisemitism they faced, and had no idea how to react to its menace.

Lastly, let us recall that Kafka did not choose the same profession as his parents. He was a lawyer and a writer. He didn't aspire to sell buttons in a haberdasher's shop, but to contribute to the *Kultur*, that important yet impalpable emanation of a people. But which people? At a moment when language was at the root of debates over identity, choosing which one to write in meant choosing a side.

* * *

Torn between multiple allegiances, none of which seemed to fit him – was he Jewish? Czech? Austrian? German? – Kafka compared himself to a man being stretched on the rack. In October 1920, one of his letters to Milena illustrated his plight with a sketch that could hardly have been more explicit: a torture device straight out of 'In the Penal Colony', which he'd written a few years earlier.

Call me arcane, but consider this: Kafka's drawing shows a man with his arms and legs outstretched to form the letter X. Cut it in two, and what do you see? Each half forms the letter K.

I don't know exactly why Kafka so insistently deprived his characters of surnames, or why he would so often give them only a single initial. It must have had something to do with the social context of the times. In 1908, political tensions between German- and Czech-speakers in Prague grew so overpowering that simply declaring yourself in favour of either language could imperil your career. The clients of the insurance company where Kafka worked were both Czech and Austrian. At the office, he would sign documents sometimes as Dr František Kafka, and sometimes as Dr Franz Kafka. František is the Czech equivalent of Franz, or Francis.

I was able to hold his birth certificate in the Bodleian Library in Oxford. It is written in two languages. Kafka possessed two versions of the same first name. One in German (Franz), and one in Czech (František). So what could he do? The plaque attached to his office door read (as did his later signatures) simply 'F. Kafka'. Not Franz, not František, just a single letter: F.

I have a similar issue with my surname. On my French passport, it says 'Hruska'; on my Czech passport, following Slavic custom, the patronym is feminised into 'Hrušková'. Thirty years after my birth, a suffix consisting of three letters and two accents is enough to cause endless problems with customs officials and bureaucrats who suspect me of identity theft.

* * *

The people around Kafka spoke Czech; but, because he was the sole addressee of Milena's letters, her Czech was able to keep all those strangers at bay. Ordinary Czech words were now enveloped in intimate connotations previously unheard, unspoken, untasted; suddenly they had meanings that he had never sensed before or elsewhere or with anyone else. If Milena had written to him in German, that would only have confirmed their geographical separation: German was the language of Vienna, not to mention the language of Milena's husband. So the Czech language dovetailed perfectly with Milena. This is what Kafka meant when he wrote: 'It is only really there [in the Czech language] that the whole Milena can be found.' Milena writing to him in German was as unbearable as it would have been if she had invited him into her marital home in Vienna. When Kafka wrote to Milena that she 'belonged' to the Czech language, really he was whispering into her ear: in Czech, you belong only to me. By writing in Czech, Milena was simultaneously leaving Vienna and cheating on her husband.

Walter Benjamin would say that the wording of their correspondence was 'pure', because it existed above language, beyond geography. And, like in Georges Bizet's *Carmen* opera, it thumbs its nose at conventions. The intimacy emitted by every page of their correspondence was neither Czech or German, but something above them, like a roof under which they could take shelter. It was their *pokoj*.

* * *

One day, when Milena told him about her husband's infidelities, Kafka feigned incomprehension: 'What is his infidelity compared to my eternal subjection!?'[8] It was a state of subjection shared by Milena, who had chosen to translate his stories into Czech almost word for word. 'I am moved by your faithfulness toward every little sentence, a faithfulness I would not have thought possible to achieve in Czech [...]. Are German and Czech so close to each other?' Kafka recognised his voice in Milena's. Rather than distancing her text from the original to adapt to the expectations of the Czech readership, Milena held it as close as she could. 'Are German and Czech so close?': Kafka's surprise returns us to Walter Benjamin's theory that translation reveals the secret affinity between two languages that, in a city like Prague, might seem irreconcilable, mutually inaudible, because they are separated by political borders.

Milena and Kafka created a meta-tongue together, a sort of linguistic airlift high above the battles raging below on earth. Kafka was amazed by it, but feared that it might come back to bite them. Would the Czech public criticise Milena for her faithfulness to a now-despised language? Might she be blamed for turns of phrase in the Czech language that sounded too Germanic, or perhaps too Jewish? 'I don't know if some

Czechs will reproach you for your fidelity, which is what I love most in your translation (not only for the story's sake, but for my own). Anyway, if someone does criticise you, try to weigh the insult against my gratitude.'

The publication of Milena's translation marks the end of what Benjamin would call the 'pure space' in which the work wavered indistinctly between Czech and German. Now the work was divided once again: the translation, for monoglot readers, appeared in Czech, while the original remained in German. And so the work descended from the 'pure' sphere, once again rooting and embodying itself in the language of the translation. In physics, this would be a 'wave function collapse', i.e. an interruption of quantum superposition. The lovers understood each other perfectly. And Franz, who could not help also being Kafka, visualised this 'pure' state as a subterranean labyrinth from which Milena would emerge alone: 'I have the feeling that I am leading you by the hand through the underground corridors – dark, base and monstrous – of the story, corridors that are almost endless (which is why my sentences are endless, don't you see?) [...] so that I will, let us hope, once we are out in the open air, have the presence of mind to disappear.' Each time Milena put down her pen after finishing her translation, it was like bringing down the theatre curtain: the monoglot reader, having access to only one language, would never know anything of the backstage area in which Kafka's language had been transformed, his words undressed then given a new costume.

'It is the nature of the visible to have an invisible lining that it makes present like an absence'. This observation, by the French philosopher Maurice Merleau-Ponty, was about paintings, but it can also be applied to translations and to love letters.[9] In the same way that the viewer standing in front of a painting sees only what the artist has made visible with his paintbrush, the reader will perceive only what the translator has heard and made audible in her own language.

Had Merleau-Ponty been a couturier, he might have illustrated his theories about the invisible lining with the image of a dress; a reversible dress that could be worn inside out. When two languages share the same mind or the same fabric, the only one to know is the woman wearing the dress against her skin. The audience can't guess at what's inside the dress. Does this kind of close cohabitation make languages resemble each other? Do I look the same if I'm wearing the dress inside out? Am I the same woman, with the same personality, depending which side of it I display? If you flip a coin and it lands heads-up, can you still glimpse the other side? The lining of a dress becomes visible only fleetingly – in a gust of wind, when I cross my legs, when I shrug my shoulder. 'Is not the most erotic portion of the body where the garment gapes?' asked Roland Barthes. The translator and the lover desire the same small opening between the visible and the invisible, the space between what is said and what is not. Ortega y Gasset compared translators to mathematicians, because 'each language is a different equation of statements and silences'.[10]

* * *

It took Kafka and Milena weeks to fix on the place, the date and the time of their next meeting. Their respective anxieties kept making them change their minds: Milena feared her husband's reaction, Kafka feared his employer's. The lovers finally agreed to meet on 15 August 1920 in Gmünd, a village whose only point of note was its location on the border of Austria and Czechoslovakia, midway between Vienna and Prague. There was something comical, almost Chaplinesque, about Gmünd's administrative ambivalence: the railway station was Czech but the village itself was Austrian. Its status was indeterminate, like the relationship between Kafka and Milena. They had to fill out form after form to be allowed to go there. Kafka, infuriated, wrote to his beloved: 'Is there no end to the stupidity of passports? Why does someone from Vienna need a passport to go through the Czech railway station? That means any inhabitants of Gmünd who want to go to Vienna must need a passport with a Czech visa, which is unbelievable. Are they doing this on purpose to annoy us?' Being in Gmünd with the correct paperwork seemed as impossible as gaining entry to the Castle.

Nobody knows what the two lovers said or did together during that getaway, but apparently it ended in disaster. The letters that followed grew less frequent, and shorter, before ceasing completely.

Their love story reached a point of no return. 'That day, we spoke to each other like strangers ...'[11] Gmünd remained irrevocably Austrian, and Kafka irrevocably Czech.

In one of his last letters, dated 1923, Kafka mentioned the years that had passed since they last said goodbye. 'I was like someone who was no longer part of this world, but I wasn't part of a new one either.' Was his relationship with Milena the only way he could connect with the world?

* * *

Kafka died on 3 June 1924 at the Kierling sanatorium, in the suburbs of Vienna. Three days later, Milena paid tribute to him in the pages of the Czech newspaper *Národní Listy*.

She informed Czech readers that Kafka, of whom they knew nothing, knew everything about them. 'He was an artist and a man of such anxious conscience he could hear even where others, deaf, felt themselves secure.' This last phrase could have been taken straight from 'The Burrow', one of his final short stories, written six months before. 'The Burrow' is like a reversed double of *The Metamorphosis*: where Gregor Samsa, man-turned-insect, is trying desperately to leave his bedroom, the narrator of 'The Burrow' shuts himself up in his to protect himself from an invisible creature that he – and no one else – can hear prowling around.[12] Milena could not have known about this story in 1924, because Max Brod waited until 1931 to publish it. Are we to conclude that Kafka and Milena had reached a space so 'pure' that they could communicate by telepathy, without need for words, even at a distance? In a letter dated 14 June 1920, Kafka told Milena about a dream he'd had: 'Your outfit, strangely, was made from the same cloth as mine.' A physicist might say that they were in a state of quantum entanglement; they instantaneously shared the same thoughts, irrespective of the language used to think them.

* * *

The Nazi laws promulgated in the 1930s in Germany, then in Austria, then in Czechoslovakia, then in most of Europe, banned the works of Kafka. Milena joined a resistance movement, helping Jews and other refugees to escape Prague.

In 1944, Milena died in Ravensbrück concentration camp.

In 1948, the Czech communist party understood Walter Benjamin's theories perfectly: since translator and author bore equal responsibility, both Milena and Kafka were banned. Where Benjamin saw an intimate language created by two beings, the censor saw a criminal conspiracy. Even within language, private property was forbidden. Kafka and Milena were dispossessed of the sole space that had ever belonged to them.

The Café Arco disappeared too, along with the writers who had patronised it. This former hotbed of Prague's Jewish-German culture now looks like an absolute non-place, requisitioned by the government and transformed into a self-service cafeteria for the Ministry of the Interior (i.e. the police force). Some rooms are so marked by the passing of time and of people that entertaining the illusion of the contrary becomes impossible.

* * *

In May 1963, to mark the eightieth anniversary of Kafka's birth, the Czech government agreed to 'rehabilitate' the writer after a meticulous international symposium held at the high-baroque Liblice Castle in the suburbs of Prague. Invited there by Eduard Goldstücker, the chairman of the Union of Czech

Writers and one of the future leaders of the Prague Spring, eighty-two specialists gathered to negotiate a truce between Kafka and Marxism–Leninism. The aim of the symposium was to rescue Kafka from his existence as a purely academic subject of study and to make his work more widely available. We can imagine the meeting a little like Rembrandt's *Anatomy Lesson*, the famous painting in which a semi-circle of surgeons dissect the corpse of an executed criminal to see what they can find.

The Soviet ideologues saw red, as they were wont to do: what gave the Czechs the right to let K into the Castle? How dare they invite this wolf (the land surveyor) into the sheepfold of socialism? This was no mere symposium – it was a political happening *disguised* as a symposium. In the official documents that would be used to justify the invasion of Czechoslovakia by Warsaw Pact troops five years later, the rehabilitation of Kafka was cited as one of the first signs of 'disobedience' paving the way for the counter-revolution.

The collected *Letters to Milena* appeared in Czech for the first time in 1968. Copies of the book were sent to be pulped on 22 August of that same year, the day after the Soviet invasion. Kafka's *Complete Works* would not appear in Czech until 2007.

* * *

In July 2023, a century after Kafka had sent his last letter to Milena, I went to the Mount Olympus of German letters, in Marbach-am-Neckar: the Deutsches Literaturarchiv – or DLA for short – where Kafka's original letters are kept.

Marbach is located twelve miles from Stuttgart, on a vine-bordered hill, at the top of which sits a turn of the nineteenth century pastiche of an eighteenth-century castle, a 1970s blockhouse, and a twenty-first-century glass gallery. In their basements is a necropolis. Together, these three buildings contain Germany's literary archives from the *Aufklärung* to the present day. It's not an ugly place – in fact, it's quite attractive – but when I arrived there, one morning in late July, everything seemed to have come to a halt. Kundera wrote somewhere that archives are the only cemetery where nobody thinks to lay flowers. I had turned up empty-handed.

* * *

The location of an archive is never insignificant. Since the time of Homer, *arkhê* – the root word for 'archive' – has meant the beginning, the commandment, the first cause. Etymologically, the archive is the primary site from which everything comes and to which everything will return. Viewed this way, the archive is a guardian of origins, a sort of literary uterus, an inaugural ground zero. The DLA was founded after the Second World War, when Germany was seeking a place to be (re)born. 'Human nature is as capable of cannibalism as it is of the *Critique of Pure Reason*.' The first part of this line, by the Austrian writer Robert Musil, has been so amply proven by history that the second part has been forgotten. The postwar German government saw an urgent need to resurrect memories of pre-Nazi Germany. For that, they brought together the nation's entire literary canon in one place, after other cannon had attempted to obliterate it all a few years earlier.

Why Marbach? Kurt Wolff, Kafka's first editor, died in a car crash there in 1963.[13] More importantly, though, the poet Friedrich Schiller was born there in 1759. My hotel, the delicatessen on the ground floor, the praline shop, the local school, the kebab stall ... all of these bear the name Schiller. He is to Marbach what Goethe is to Weimar, Pushkin to St Petersburg, Dante to Florence, and Erasmus to Rotterdam: a mascot. Besides, postwar Germany was not exactly overflowing with historically or politically neutral places. Weimar, where Goethe spent most of his life, was now part of East Germany. Bonn and Berlin had too many unwelcome connotations. Munich? Don't even think about it. Hamburg? You've got to be kidding. Dresden? Well, that would be a strange setting for a resurrection.

The DLA was inaugurated in 1955 with a speech given by Thomas Mann on the one hundred and fiftieth anniversary of Schiller's death. Germany had been cut in two, and Mann, by then an American citizen and Swiss resident, had not lived in his homeland for more than twenty years. So why him? Mann was the archetype – another word derived from *arkhê* – of the German in exile. While Marbach obviously could not reunite West and East Germany, at least it could act as a bridge between the pre-1933 and post-1933 nation. There, archivists repatriated and organised the manuscripts of writers who had been banned, killed or exiled by the Nazi regime, whether they were German or not.[14] This is why Kafka does not stand out as an orphan or a foreigner here, but seems in good company. Hofmannsthal, Rilke, Arendt, Roth, Kafka: until 1955, their archives had been as scattered as their lives. With the DLA, Marbach became their home and German the language of their homecoming.

'Let your language be for you what the body is for lovers. It alone separates beings and unites them': so ran the motto of the literary magazine founded by Schiller and Goethe. In Marbach, these words have a practical significance.

* * *

At my hotel, I'm greeted by the chambermaid, who introduces herself to me as 'Monika'. 'I came here just for you,' she tells me. 'You're our only guest this week. What brings you here in the middle of summer?' We chat for a few minutes in German. I mention Kafka and the book that I am thinking of writing. She stops me: 'Kafka?' Monika assures me she knows this man's writing. But the word she uses is 'Handschrift' – his handwriting. She is quite categorical: she would recognise his calligraphy among those of a thousand other men. Not a bad party trick.

When she arrived in Germany from the Balkans about thirty years ago, Monika was hired as a cleaner 'over there', she says, gesturing with her eyes towards the hill. Back then, some of Kafka's manuscripts were on public display, behind glass. 'I had to spray-clean the glass every two hours – it was always filthy.' The writings were exposed to visitors' fingerprints, condensed breath and gobs of spit. Monika mimes pulling the trigger of the cleaning spray. When she imitates Kafka's handwriting, she doesn't wave her arms about like an orchestra conductor, but makes jerky little wrist movements, her head tilted to one side. I think about *The Metamorphosis*: in that story, the only character to show any sympathy towards Gregor after his transformation into an insect is the cleaning lady employed by the Samsa family. Every day, she goes into his bedroom to ventilate it, leaving the windows open, giving Gregor a chance to escape.

* * *

Inevitably, Kafka's archives are subject to bureaucratic interference. Access to the manuscripts, in Marbach or in Oxford (one of three main archives of his papers),[15] requires forms, authorisations, files, photocopies, letters, exemptions, long waiting periods, proof of qualifications and identity. Back then, not having written a single line of this book, all I had to offer were blank pages. Another source of suspicion was the fact that I was not a historian or a linguist or a PhD student or attached to any academic institution.

'Couldn't you make do with our high-resolution copies on your computer?' I was asked. 'No,' I replied. If Tintin was justifiably anxious, in *Tintin and the Broken Ear*, about the growing number of Arumbaya statuettes in an ocean of terracotta copies, surely I was entitled to reject the idea of Kafka's writings dissolving into the digital cloud. I wanted to meet this man face-to-face. 'Our reproductions are extremely high-quality,' I was told. 'In even the most perfect reproduction, *one* thing is lacking: the here and now of the work of art – its unique existence in a particular place.' The woman looked nonplussed. It's Walter Benjamin, I added earnestly. She sighed and nodded. 'Well, okay, then. Come with me.'

KAFKA AND MILENA JESENSKÁ

* * *

In the manuscripts room, there are no clocks, no phone reception, no toilets, no noise, no daylight. Benjamin would say that archive rooms represent 'a strange tissue of space and time' because neither are present there. Kafka's letters and postcards are in such perfect condition that I ask the archivists – identifiable by their white coats, and horrified by my question – if these really are the originals. The postmarks look freshly inked, and the paper is neither crumpled nor yellowed. The words have not faded in the slightest. Kafka wrote his initials in such a way that the lines at the top of the F and the K seem to reach out their arms to the recipient. These letters are not addressed to me, but they are so immaculate that I feel as if a postman has just delivered them into my hands.

* * *

There is nothing dusty about the Marbach archives. In almost a century of study, Kafka's letters to Milena have been touched, X-rayed, catalogued and retranscribed by researchers. What was I expecting from these originals? A revelation, or perhaps a confession? An apparition? I try to spot the difference between these originals and the transcriptions sold in bookshops. I'm not going to find anything as obvious as in the children's game (an ink blot here, a smudge there, a doodle at the bottom of a page), but I am looking for *something*: an infinitesimal breach into which I might crawl.

The archive is not virginal, of course, but I am seeing it with my own eyes for the very first time. I am hoping to find some small detail that might have escaped the attention of all the eyes that have been here before mine. I look up at the readers around me. Some are standing, hands gripping the table as they lean over their papers, staring intensely at the texts. With its stark fluorescent lighting, the manuscripts room has the feel of an interrogation cell. It has its own ways of making you speak ...

The etymology of the word 'search' gives up its secrets easily: it comes from the Latin *circare*, which means 'to go round', like pilgrims going around a black cube, like circus animals parading at the centre of a big top, like K circling the Castle. The historian Jules Michelet wrote of the archives' 'galvanic dance'. I imagine this manuscripts room like the boy's bedroom in *Toy Story*, but the archives are inert when nobody is here; they come to life only under the gaze of someone who truly desires to meet them.

* * *

To protect them from the lips and fingertips of overly passionate believers, orthodox icons are usually covered with a thin layer of metal. At the DLA, some of the letters are behind glass. Others are wrapped in tissue, and kept in a cardboard folder, inside a cold room, located on the third basement floor of a blockhouse, reinforced by digital locks and fire-resistant doors.

Looking at these letters, I believe I am in the presence of what Benjamin called the 'aura' of a work. What is this aura? Not a poltergeist knocking on the table, but something more subtle and compelling. Put simply, you don't approach Kafka's manuscripts the way you might study a paperback book, even if the paperback perfectly reproduced the look and substance of the originals. Benjamin defined the aura as 'the unique apparition of a distance'. Expressed in those terms, the phrase seems too abstract. I didn't understand it until later, when I was reading Kafka's diaries, which are kept in the Bodleian Library in Oxford. The librarian handed me a notebook wrapped in protective paper. 'Gently hold the spine with your palm,' he said. A curious choice of words, I thought. And yet his gestures were so delicate that I half-expected him to hand me a swaddled newborn. So what is aura, then? The fear – when faced with an inert yet radiant, antique object that does not belong to you – of hurting it irreparably.

Like his diaries, Kafka's letters to Milena still exist only thanks to a series of haloed coincidences. Sent from Prague, Vienna and various sanatoriums in the Tyrol, these letters might have disappeared a hundred times over, destroyed by their author or their recipient or by the Gestapo, or simply lost in the post. While the world was darkening around her, while German troops were encircling Prague, Milena, knowing that she faced imminent deportation, gave the letters to her friend Willy Haas. The founder of the magazine *Literarische Welt*, to which Walter Benjamin contributed, Haas kept them safe throughout his wartime exile in India. Did those letters already possess an aura, in Milena's eyes? Did they, for her, represent the unique apparition of a distant love? Perhaps she imagined being able to show them to her children one day. See how loved your mother was, when she was young.

* * *

These letters are a hundred years old, but they are still alive. You could even characterise them as survivors, since they bear witness to a history that threatened them with destruction. Primo Levi would sometimes say that the expression 'a witness of history' made no sense: the simple fact of having survived an event in some way prevented you from bearing witness to it. Paul Celan, another Kafka translator, distilled this insight into a line of verse, *Ashglory*: 'Niemand zeugt *für den Zeugen*' – 'No one bears witness for the witness'. The letters to Milena are like this: they do not bear witness to history. On the contrary, they completely elude history. They belong to a space that is intimate, awe-inspiring, impregnable, 'pure'. They belong to that parallel world for which only Milena and Kafka ever possessed the key. Their *pokoj*.

Epilogue

We are born, so to speak, provisionally,
it doesn't matter where; it is only gradually that
we compose, within ourselves, our true place
of origin, so that we may be born there
retrospectively, and each day more definitely.

    Rainer Maria Rilke, letter to Duchess Aurelia Gallarati Scotti (1923)

In his 1977 novel *The Professor of Desire*, Philip Roth sent his avatar, David Kepesh, on a journey across Europe. In Prague, Kepesh visits the Strašnice cemetery and stands in front of Kafka's grave. As far as we know, Kafka had no descendants, and in 1977 he was still *persona non grata* in Czechoslovakia, the location of his grave not shown on any maps. And yet, as Kepesh observes, his tombstone is the best kept in the graveyard.

Strašnice, a neighbourhood at the crossroads of what Robert Musil called the 'old axes of the world', is home to three cemeteries. Vladimir Nabokov was barred from attending his own mother's funeral in 1939 in one of them, the same cemetery where my grandparents are buried. My grandmother's name was Ludmilla Kafka. I have never been able to work out whether her maiden name was just a happy coincidence. All the schools she attended until adolescence were German-speaking. When did she learn Czech? And how, with that surname, was she able to live in Bohemia during the 1930s and 1940s? Did she find a way to hide her *pokoj*, and keep her secrets? Sadly, I never thought to ask her.

I was overwhelmed by the passing of my grandparents. Particularly since they were followed by another loss for which I was not prepared: that of the apartment, in the Žižkov neighbourhood, that our family had rented for four generations. My grandparents had lived there with their own parents, their children and their grandchildren. Altogether, they occupied those rooms for almost a century. My grandfather had been born there in 1931. Towards the end of his life, despite his blindness, he would move around the apartment with incredible ease, like Borges in the corridors of the Buenos Aires library. His hands knew the way. He carried that space inside him, and that space carried him through life. It was his *pokoj*, and it was part of mine too.

When they died, we had to hastily pack up that world, or what remained of it, and move out. The landlord wanted us out of there quickly. But where were we supposed to start packing up? At which end? In 1984, when the French translation of his novel *The Unbearable Lightness of Being* was published, Milan Kundera was interviewed by the journalist Bernard Pivot, who gestured at the book's cover, then said: 'It's not easy to know which end of your story we should tackle first.' Kundera replied: 'That's because there are a lot of ends.'

The same was true for my grandparents' apartment, the story of which is difficult to unravel. 'Vyhod' to co nemá duši,' my great-aunt advised me: 'Start by throwing away what has no soul.' Easier said than done. Sadness – and grief especially – can make an animist of anyone. The most insignificant knick-knack seems charged with existential density. Pick up any object, and it comes to life at the precise moment that you imagine separating yourself from it.

Nothing that appears to be ours or a part of our life is invulnerable to the possibility of a theft, a crash, an expulsion, a disaster. *Everything you don't possess will be taken from you.* That message was hammered into me as a child: I had to build something impregnable, a place that could, in an emergency, be folded away, buried, dematerialised, and redeployed elsewhere. This is the place that I call my *pokoj*. For me, it is the mental equivalent of a Swiss safe-deposit box. It can pass through walls and cross borders without being confiscated by customs officials. My *pokoj* is like the place where Gregor Samsa, waking up after his metamorphosis, gathers his thoughts, while everything that he had until then considered certain and consubstantial – his appearance, his voice, his relationships with members of his family – collapses under him. 'His room, a proper human room, although a little too small, lay peacefully between its four familiar walls.' I continue thinking my way around the Žižkov apartment, *between its four famil-*

iar walls, as if there existed a door between my *pokoj* and my grandparents' *pokoj*. A 'communicating' doorframe, as an architect would call it.

As insignificant as the loss of part of my *pokoj* may be when set against the world's vast tragedies, it is possible that the affinities I feel for Kafka's first translators spring from that separation. Josef K, the land surveyor, Gregor Samsa, Karl Rossmann, the trapeze artist: what Kafka's translators have in common with his characters is that they were all, one day, torn from the place that had nurtured their relationship with their language and with the world.

I believe I must have I sensed the echo of that loss in their respective works, just as Kafka's translators had sensed in his writing a resonance with their own lives. Their loss could not be reversed, but, under close examination, it could be illuminated.

The *pokoj* feeds on the questions it stumbles upon. That is why it's not a bunker, but a space that expands as our view of what is happening outside it becomes clearer.

Like the ninety-nine narrators who, in Raymond Queneau's *Exercises in Style* (1947), tell the same story in ninety-nine different ways, each of Kafka's translators has their own way of seeing, feeling, understanding, interpreting. If they were all invited around a table to discuss the author they had in common, or if they were summoned to a courtroom to defend him, would those translators feel as if they were all talking about the same man? Probably not.

The ten versions of Kafka presented in this book, like the various *pokoje* from which they emerged, are at once convergent and divergent. Kafka is revealed through the distorting lens of these ten translators, who project their own light upon him while absorbing the light he emits. His many afterlives find their most convincing form in the colossal kinetic sculpture of his head by the artist David Černý in Prague. Sliced into horizontal strips, Kafka's face remains still even while these mechanised strips rotate constantly, at different speeds, some clockwise, some anticlockwise, never in the same direction, but always around the same axis. In this way, perfect alignment becomes structurally impossible.

The more we try to fix him with our gaze, the more Kafka eludes us.

Acknowledgements

In a letter dated 9 November 1903, Kafka wrote to his friend Oskar Pollak, as follows: 'For me, you were, along with much else, also something like a window through which I could see the streets. I could not do that for myself, for tall though I am I do not yet reach to the windowsill.'

These words are for the people who, through their affection and generous erudition, enabled me to reach that 'window' and shine some new light into my chapters. This book owes them a debt of gratitude.

My thanks go, firstly, to my French publishers, Grasset. To my editor Pauline Perrignon, who used all her intelligence and sensitivity to help this book develop from its early stages, through numerous reworkings, to its final form.

To Olivier Nora for his trust and his immense chic.

To Charles Dantzig for his valuable reading of the chapter on Alexandre Vialatte.

To Agnès Nivière for her endless patience.

I would also like to express my deep gratitude to:

Sonia Feertchak and Sven Ortoli, whose friendship and sharp minds are a constant source of inspiration.

Ulysse Manhes, the most perceptive of readers, for his stimulating bibliographical discoveries and his invitations to talk through many of the ideas developed in this book.

Constance Perret-Bertrandias, Sylvie Adler, Laurence Kuznetsov, Edouard Machover, Mikaël Guthart-Gomez, Lakis Proguidis, Leopold de Stabenrath, and Yoel Gamzou for their generous advice and their attentive listening.

Malgorzata Czepiel, curator of Franz Kafka's manuscripts at the Bodleian Library in Oxford, and the staff of the Deutsches Literaturarchiv in Marbach-am-Neckar, for their kindness and assistance.

Sarah Chalfant and Andrew Wylie, for their constant support and their high standards in all things.

My brother, Hugo Hruska, for his energy and his unwavering encouragements.

My parents, who will guess how much this book owes to them.

I also wish to express my endless admiration to Sam Taylor, whose own 'version' of *Dix Versions de Kafka* has enhanced the original in every possible way. The dedication and care of his rendition have far exceeded

ACKNOWLEDGEMENTS

everything I had hoped for – elegantly illustrating the very thing I so laboriously sought to convey in this book.

My deepest thanks also extend to my editors Eva Hodgkin and Gabriella Doob who saw a place for this book with English readers and welcomed it to their UK and US publishing homes respectively.

This book is finally indebted to Freya Alsop, Kit Shepherd and all their dedicated colleagues at William Collins and Ecco Press whose masterful hands and rigorous minds have graced these pages.

Notes

Kafka: In the Land of the Soviets

1. In French, *une grande hache* can mean both 'a big axe' and 'a capital H' (translator's note).
2. This was Milan Kundera's view of Kafka's prophetic tendencies, as expressed in *The Art of the Novel* (1986): that, since public life was governed by the same laws as private life, one need only observe what is happening at home to grasp what is going on in the outside world.
3. These terms are taken from Michael Löwy's study of the sociology of organisations in the works of Kafka, entitled 'Paper Chains: Bureaucratic Despotism and Voluntary Servitude in Franz Kafka's *The Castle*', published in *Diogène*, no. 204 (2003/4).

4. This scene is described in Laure Murat's *Proust, roman familial* (2023).
5. Diary entry from July 1916: 'Impossible to live with F [Felice]. Impossibility of sharing my life with anyone. No regrets.'
6. This observation was made by Michel Carrouges, quoted in Georges Bataille, *Literature and Evil* (1957).

Kafka and Eugene Jolas: The East–West Translation

1. Nabokov's words are from an appreciation of the exiled Russian poet Vladimir Hodasevich written shortly after his death in Paris in 1939, reprinted in *Verses and Versions: Three Centuries of Russian Poetry Selected and Translated by Vladimir Nabokov*, ed. Brian Bond and Stanislav Shvabrin (2008).
2. These words are from *The Gift*, a novel written in Berlin in 1937 and published in Paris in 1938. The book is a sort of farewell to the Russian language. The following year, Nabokov would leave for the United States and adopt the English language.
3. Pierre Nora defines a realm of memory as 'any significant entity, whether material or non-material in nature, which by dint of human will or the work of time has become a symbolic element of the memorial heritage of any community'.

Kafka and Jorge Luis Borges: Two Men in a Labyrinth

1. The occasionally arbitrary reorganisation that Max Brod imposed on his friend's texts was severely condemned by (among others) Hannah Arendt, who reproached him for the numerous cuts he had made, removing any clues that might have helped us understand the writer's creative process.
2. Jorge Luis Borges, 'The Homeric Versions' (1932).
3. He was removed from his position in 1946, following President Juan Perón's accession to power.
4. From Borges' preface to his translation of *The Metamorphosis* (1938).
5. Jorge Luis Borges, 'The Other', in *The Book of Sand* (1975), quoted in Roland Béhar, '"Être Kafka": Borges et le rêve d'un autre lui-même', in Roland Béhar and Annick Louis (ed.), *Lire Borges aujourd'hui: Autour de 'Ficciones' et 'El Hacedor'* (2016).
6. It inspired others too: there is a character in Umberto Eco's *The Name of the Rose* (1980) – a blind and capricious librarian – named Jorge de Burgos.
7. Bartleby is the eponymous protagonist of Herman Melville's short story 'Bartleby, the Scrivener' (1853). Employed by a lawyer on Wall Street, Bartleby replies to all his boss's requests simply: 'I would prefer not to.'

Kafka and Paul Celan: The Balm and the Wound

1. Quoted by Nicole Lapierre, *Pensons ailleurs* (2004).
2. The other three volumes consist of his unpublished and posthumous texts; what Alexandre Vialatte called a 'book of sweepings', a collection of the crumbs fallen from the writer's table. Loose sheets of paper, unfinished fragments, that Celan had kept in a folder bearing the instruction 'DO NOT PUBLISH'. His last wishes betrayed: something else he had in common with Kafka.
3. Paul Celan, 'The Meridian' (1960).
4. Emil Cioran, 'The Advantages of Exile', in his *The Temptation to Exist* (1956).
5. Celan, 'The Meridian'.
6. Levi would later acknowledge, in his anthology *The Search for Roots*, that he carried Celan's 'Death Fugue' around inside him like a 'transplanted organ'.

Kafka and Melech Ravitch: What Have You Done to Your Brother?

1. Quoted in Annette Wieviorka, *The Era of the Witness* (2006).
2. After the 1905 Revolution, the tsarist government announced a raft of antisemitic laws, supposedly

because they considered the Jews largely responsible for the disorder in the empire's great cities.
3. Quoted in Klaus Wagenbach, *Franz Kafka: les années de jeunesse (1883–1912)* (1967).
4. The well-known satirical reworking by Nicolas Chamfort (1741–94) of the French Revolution's slogan 'Fraternity or Death'.

Kafka and Primo Levi: The Recurring Nightmare

1. Quoted in Georges Didi-Huberman, *Images in Spite of All* (2003).
2. This passage is based on Didi-Huberman's analysis of 'the unthinkable' and 'the incommunicable' in *Images in Spite of All*, to which this entire chapter is greatly indebted.
3. Primo Levi, 'Translating Kafka', in *The Mirror Maker* (1989).
4. Perhaps this was Calvino's way of helping Einaudi redeem itself, the publishing house – then under the direction of Cesare Pavese and Natalia Ginzburg – having rejected the manuscript of *If This Is a Man* thirty-five years earlier.
5. An episode recounted in Levi's *The Drowned and the Saved* (1986).
6. The meeting between author and translator is described by Myriam Anissimov in her biography, *Primo Levi: Tragedy of an Optimist* (1998). Levi

also learned that Riedt had been a resistance fighter, and that they shared the same birthday.

Kafka and Alexandre Vialatte: Make Me Laugh

1. As noted by Éric Faye in 1996.
2. As noted by Tzvetan Todorov in *The Fantastic* (1970).
3. A new Pléiade edition of the *Complete Works*, retranslated by Jean-Pierre Lefebvre, was published in 2022.

Kafka and Bruno Schulz: If Walls Could Talk

1. 'Prague won't let us go. […] This little mother has claws.' Franz Kafka, letter to Oskar Pollak, 20 December 1902.
2. Exiled in Paris since 1933, Roth lived in hotels on Rue de Tournon, near the Senate, a neighbourhood he affectionately nicknamed 'the Republic of Tournon'.
3. Max Brod published the first edition of *The Trial* in 1925, followed by *The Castle* in 1926 and *Amerika* in 1927.
4. This information is taken from *Regions of the Great Heresy* (2003), a biography of Schulz written by Jerzy Ficowski, who was the equivalent, in Schulz's posthumous literary career, of Max Brod in Kafka's. He gathered Schulz's drawings and

writings for publication, in addition to telling his life story. The current chapter as a whole is largely based on Ficowski's book, as well as a more recent, and highly enlightening, biography by Benjamin Balint, *Bruno Schulz: An Artist, a Murder, and the Hijacking of History* (2023).
5. Published in Ernst Klee, Willi Dressen and Volker Riess (eds), *'The Good Old Days': The Holocaust as Seen by Its Perpetrators and Bystanders* (1991).
6. Ian Traynor, 'Murals Illuminate Holocaust Legacy Row', *Guardian*, 2 July 2001.
7. Andrew Meier, 'Whose Art Is It Anyway?', *Time*, 16 July 2001.
8. The synagogue was restored at last only in 2018.
9. *Yad Vashem* means literally 'a monument and a name', and is taken from a verse in the Bible: 'I will give in my house and within my walls a monument and a name [...] that shall not be cut off' (Isaiah 56:5, English Standard Version).
10. Benjamin Balint's excellent book already cited describes the fate of these murals and how it relates to geopolitical and remembrance issues.

Kafka and Hebrew: The Promised Translation

1. Kafka, *Diaries*, entry for 12 September 1912.
2. The Czernowitz Congress of 1908 had declared Yiddish the 'national language of the diaspora' on the grounds that 'Hebrew was the national

language of the past, Yiddish the national language of the present', according to the linguist Mateusz Mieses.
3. In 2010, the literary critic George Steiner quoted these words from the Talmud: 'The omission or the addition of one letter might mean the destruction of the whole world.'
4. Posthumously published in 1931 in the collection *The Great Wall of China*. Is the story's title a reference to Prague's coat of arms, which showed not one tower, but three?
5. Described in Marek Nekula, *Franz Kafka and His Prague Contexts* (2016).
6. This body replaced the Hebrew Language Committee, established in 1889.
7. The story of Kafka's translations into Hebrew is wonderfully and comprehensively recounted by Benjamin Balint in *Kafka's Last Trial: The Strange Case of a Literary Legacy* (2018).
8. George Steiner, *Language and Silence: Essays on Language, Literature, and the Inhuman* (1967).

Kafka and Milena Jesenská: A Love of Translation

1. A line quoted in Adonis and Houria Abdelouahed, *Le Regard d'Orphée* (2009).
2. Paul Valéry, *Cahiers*, ed. Judith Robinson (1973).
3. The circle of Jewish-German writers in Prague included Max Brod, Johannes Urzidil, Franz

Werfel, Egon Erwin Kisch and Oskar Baum. The Viennese polemicist Karl Kraus nicknamed them, no doubt disparagingly, the 'Arconauts'.
4. A not insignificant word, since it means 'root' in Czech.
5. Kafka, *Letters to Milena*, 24 July 1920.
6. The 1871 law guaranteeing legal equality for the two languages had been repealed.
7. Kafka, *Letters to Milena*, 28 July 1920.
8. Kafka, *Letters to Milena*, 13 August 1920.
9. Maurice Merleau-Ponty, 'Eye and Mind' (1961).
10. José Ortega y Gasset, 'The Misery and the Splendor of Translation' (1937).
11. Kafka, *Letters to Milena*, 20 August 1920.
12. With remarkable irony, an extract from 'The Burrow' appeared a few years later in the Czech magazine *Svetova Literatura* (literally: 'Literature of the World'). So Kafka, who had spent his entire life in Prague, found himself published in a Prague magazine devoted to foreign literature.
13. Kurt Wolff and his wife Helen fled Nazi Germany and moved to New York, where they founded Pantheon Books with Jacques Schiffrin. Kurt Wolff had joined the publishing house Rowohlt, founded by Ernst Rowohlt, in 1908.
14. The DLA also houses the editorial collections of major German publishing houses, including those of the magazine *Aufbau* (meaning 'Construction/ Reconstruction' in English) which was founded in

New York and became the most important weekly for German writers in exile.
15. Kafka's manuscripts are divided between archives in Marbach, Oxford and Jerusalem.

Bibliography

During the past century, biographers, essayists, exegetes and editors have produced a valuable collection of documents relating to Kafka and the translators featured in this book. I am grateful to them for having made the works and lives of my subjects more accessible.

Adorno, Theodor W., *Negative Dialectics*, tr. E. B. Ashton (Continuum, 1973).
Alazraki, Jaime (ed.), *Critical Essays on Jorge Luis Borges* (G. K. Hall, 1987).
Amigorena, Santiago, *The Ghetto Within*, tr. Frank Wynne (HarperVia, 2022).
Anders, Günther, *L'Émigré*, tr. Armand Croissant (Allia, 2022).
——, *Journaux de l'exil et du retour*, tr. Isabelle Kalinowski (Éditions Fage, 2012).

———, *Nous, fils d'Eichmann*, tr. Sabine Cornille and Philippe Ivernel (Rivages, 2003).

Anissimov, Myriam, *Primo Levi: Tragedy of an Optimist*, tr. Steve Cox (The Overlook Press, 2000).

Appelfeld, Aharon, *L'Héritage nu (Au-delà du désespoir)*, tr. Michel Gribinski (Éditions de L'Olivier, 2022).

———, *The Story of a Life: A Memoir*, tr. Aloma Halter (Schocken Books, 2004).

Arendt, Hannah, *Auschwitz et Jérusalem*, tr. Sylvie Courtine-Denamy (Pocket, 1998).

———, *Cahier Hannah Arendt*, ed. Martine Leibovici and Aurore Mréjen (L'Herne, 'Cahiers de L'Herne', 2021).

———, *Eichmann in Jerusalem: A Report on the Banality of Evil* (Penguin, 2022).

———, *La Tradition cachée: le Juif comme paria*, tr. Sylvie Courtine-Denamy (Payot, 2019).

Arendt, Hannah, and Karl Jaspers, *Correspondence, 1926–1969*, ed. Lotte Kohler and Hans Saner, tr. Robert and Rita Kimber (Harcourt Brace, 1992).

Balint, Benjamin, *Bruno Schulz: An Artist, a Murder, and the Hijacking of History* (W. W. Norton, 2023).

———, *Kafka's Last Trial: The Strange Case of a Literary Legacy* (W. W. Norton, 2018).

Barthes, Roland, *The Pleasure of the Text*, tr. Richard Miller (Hill and Wang, 1975).

Bashevis Singer, Isaac, *Shadows on the Hudson*, tr. Joseph Sherman (Farrar, Straus and Giroux, 1998).

Bataille, Georges, *Literature and Evil*, tr. Alastair Hamilton (Penguin, 2012).

Bechtel, Delphine, *La Renaissance culturelle juive en Europe centrale et orientale, 1897–1930: langue, littérature et construction nationale* (Belin, 2002).

Béhar, Roland and Annick, Louis (eds), *Lire Borges aujourd'hui: Autour de 'Ficciones' et 'El Hacedor'* (Éditions Rue d'Ulm, 2016).

Benjamin, Walter, 'On Some Motifs in Baudelaire' (1840), tr. Harry Zohn, in *Selected Writings, Volume 4: 1938–1940*, ed. Howard Eiland and Michael W. Jennings (Belknap Press, 2003).

——, 'The Task of the Translator' (1923), tr. Harry Zohn, in *Selected Writings, Volume 1: 1913–1926*, ed. Marcus Bullock and Michael W. Jennings (Belknap Press, 1996).

——, 'The Work of Art in the Age of Its Technological Reproducibility: Second Version' (1935–6), tr. Edmond Jephcott and Harry Zohn, in *Selected Writings, Volume 3: 1935–1938*, ed. Howard Eiland and Michael W. Jennings (Belknap Press, 2002).

——, 'The Work of Art in the Age of Mechanical Reproduction' (1939), in *Illuminations*, tr. Harry Zohn (Harcourt Brace, 1968).

Berlin, Isaiah, 'The Origins of Israel' (1953), in *The Power of Ideas*, ed. Henry Hardy (Princeton University Press, 2000).

Berman, Antoine, *The Experience of the Foreign: Culture and Translation in Romantic Germany*, tr. S. Heyvaert (State University of New York Press, 1992).

Besson, Ferny, *Alexandre Vialatte ou la complainte d'un enfant frivole* (JC Lattès, 1999).

Blanchot, Maurice, *De Kafka à Kafka* (Gallimard, 'Folio', 1981).

Borges, Jorge Luis, 'An Autobiographical Essay', in *The Aleph and Other Stories, 1933–1969*, ed. and tr. Norman Thomas di Giovanni (Dutton, 1970).

——, *Collected Fictions*, tr. Andrew Hurley (Penguin, 1999).

——, 'The Homeric Versions' (1932), in *The Total Library: Non-Fiction, 1922–1986*, ed. Eliot Weinberger, tr. Esther Allen et al. (Penguin, 1999).

——, *Labyrinths: Selected Stories and Other Writings*, ed. Donald A. Yates and James E. Irby (New Directions, 1964).

——, *Livre de préfaces/Essai Autobiographique*, tr. Françoise Rosset and Michel Seymour Tripier (Gallimard, 'Folio', 1987).

——, *Selected Poems*, ed. Alexander Coleman (Penguin, 1999).

Bourcet-Rousseaux, Pascale, 'Une hostile parenté: les relations contrastées de Rilke à Prague', in Maurice Godé et al., *Allemands, Juifs et Tchèques à Prague, 1890–1924* (Presses universitaires de la Méditerranée, 1996).

Bourel, Dominique, *Martin Buber: Sentinelle de l'humanité* (Albin Michel, 2015).

Brodsky, Joseph, *Collected Poems in English*, ed. Ann Kjelleberg (Farrar, Straus and Giroux, 2000).

——, 'Flight from Byzantium', in *The New Yorker*, 20 October 1985.

——, 'In a Room and a Half', in *Less than One: Selected Essays* (Farrar, Straus and Giroux, 1986).

Buber, Martin, *I and Thou*, tr. Ronald Gregor Smith (Scribner, 2000).

Caillois, Roger, *Borges: thèmes fondamentaux* (Fata Morgana, 2009).

Camus, Albert, *The Myth of Sisyphus*, tr. Justin O'Brien (Vintage, 2018).

Canetti, Elias, *The Memoirs of Elias Canetti: The Tongue Set Free, The Torch in My Ear, The Play of the Eyes*, tr. Joachim Neugroschel and Ralph Manheim (Farrar, Straus and Giroux, 1999).

Celan, Paul, *The Meridian: Final Version – Drafts – Materials*, ed. Bernhard Böschenstein et al., tr. Pierre Joris (Stanford University Press, 2011).

——, *No One's Rose*, tr. David Young (Marick Press, 2014).

——, *Selected Poems and Prose*, tr. John Felstiner (W. W. Norton, 2001)

——, *Selections*, tr. Pierre Joris (University of California Press, 2005).

Chenot, Aurélie, *Colombey est une fête* (Éditions Inculte, 2022).

Cioran, Emil, *Cahiers, 1957–1972* (Gallimard, 1997).
——, *On the Heights of Despair*, tr. Ilinca Zarifopol-Johnston (University of Chicago Press, 1992).
——, *The Temptation to Exist*, tr. Richard Howard (Arcade, 2013).
Clair, Jean, 'La Chambre double', *Revue des Deux Mondes*, May 2017.
Courtine-Denamy, Sylvie, *L'Exil dans l'exil: les langues de l'ailleurs, l'ailleurs des langues* (Hermann, 2014).
David, Yasha, and Jean-Pierre Morel (eds), *Le Siècle de Kafka*, exhibition catalogue (Centre Georges-Pompidou, 1984).
Derrida, Jacques, *Monolingualism of the Other, or, The Prosthesis of Origin*, tr. Patrick Mensah (Stanford University Press, 1998).
——, *Les Yeux de la langue: l'abîme et le volcan* (Galilée, 2012).
Didi-Huberman, Georges, *Images in Spite of All*, tr. Shane B. Lillis (University of Chicago Press, 2012).
——, *Le Témoin jusqu'au bout: une lecture de Victor Klemperer* (Minuit, 2022).
Faye, Éric, *Le Sanatorium des malades du temps: attente et fiction autour de Julien Gracq, Dino Buzzati, Thomas Mann, Kôbô Abé* (Éditions José Corti, 1996).
Ficowski, Jerzy, *Regions of the Great Heresy: Bruno Schulz, a Biographical Portrait*, tr. and ed. Theodosia Robertson (W. W. Norton & Co., 2003).
Finkielkraut, Alain, *The Defeat of the Mind*, tr. Judith Friedlander (Columbia University Press, 1995).

Gombrowicz, Witold, *Moi et mon double*, tr. Christian Bourgois (Gallimard, 'Quarto', 1996).

——, *Polish Memories*, tr. Bill Johnston (Yale University Press, 2004).

Gouri, Haïm, *Facing the Glass Booth: The Jerusalem Trial of Adolf Eichmann*, tr. Michael Swirsky (Wayne State University Press, 2004).

Herzl, Theodor, *The Jewish State (Der Judenstaat)*, tr. Harry Zohn (Herzl Press, 1970).

Janouch, Gustav, *Conversations with Kafka*, tr. Goronwy Rees (New Directions, 2012).

Jesenská, Milena, *The Journalism of Milena Jesenská: A Critical Voice in Interwar Central Europe*, ed. and tr. Kathleen Hayes (Berghahn Books, 2003).

Jolas, Eugene, *Man from Babel*, ed. Andreas Kramer and Rainer Rumold (Yale University Press, 1998).

Kafka, Franz, *Amerika*, tr. Willa and Edwin Muir (Penguin, 1974).

——, *The Castle*, ed. Ritchie Robertson, tr. Anthea Bell (Oxford University Press, 2009).

——, *The Complete Stories*, ed. Nahum Glatzer, tr. Willa and Edwin Muir, and Tania and James Stern (Schocken Books, 1971).

——, *Dearest Father: Stories and Other Writings*, tr. Ernst Kaiser and Eithne Wilkins (Schocken Books, 1954).

——, *The Description of a Struggle*, tr. Tania and James Stern (Schocken Books, 1958).

——, *The Diaries of Franz Kafka, 1910–23*, ed. Max Brod, tr. Joseph Kresh, Martin Greenberg and Hannah Arendt (Penguin, 1972).
——, *The Diaries*, tr. Ross Benjamin (Schocken Books, 2022).
——, *The Great Wall of China and Other Pieces*, tr. Willa and Edwin Muir (Secker and Warburg, 1946).
——, *Letters to Felice*, ed. Erich Heller and Jürgen Born, tr. James Stern and Elisabeth Duckworth (Schocken Books, 1973).
——, *Letters to Friends, Family and Editors*, tr. Richard and Clara Winston (Knopf, 1990).
——, *Letters to Milena*, ed. Willy Haas, tr. Tania and James Stern (Schocken Books, 1953).
——, *Letters to Milena*, tr. Philip Boehm (Schocken Books, 2015).
——, *Metamorphosis*, tr. David Wyllie (2002).
——, *The Trial*, tr. David Wyllie (2003).
Kessel, Joseph, *Jugements Derniers: les Procès Pétain, de Nuremberg et Eichmann* (Tallandier, 2018).
Klee, Ernst, Willi Dressen and Volker Riess (eds), *'The Good Old Days': The Holocaust as Seen by Its Perpetrators and Bystanders*, tr. Deborah Burnstone (Konecky and Konecky, 1991).
Kristal, Efraín, *Invisible Work: Borges and Translation* (Vanderbilt University Press, 2002).
Kundera, Milan, *The Art of the Novel*, tr. Linda Asher (Grove Press, 1988).

——, *The Book of Laughter and Forgetting*, tr. Aaron Asher (HarperCollins, 1996).

——, *89 Words followed by Prague, A Disappearing Poem*, tr. Matt Reeck (Harper, 2025).

——, *A Kidnapped West: The Tragedy of Central Europe*, tr. Linda Asher and Edmund White (Harper, 2023).

——, *Life Is Elsewhere*, tr. Aaron Asher (HarperCollins, 2000).

——, *Œuvre*, tr. Marcel Aymonin, François Kérel and Eva Bloch, 2 vols (Gallimard, 'Bibliothèque de la Pléiade', 2011).

——, *Testaments Betrayed: An Essay in Nine Parts*, tr. Linda Asher (HarperCollins, 1995).

——, *The Unbearable Lightness of Being*, tr. Michael Henry Heim (Faber and Faber, 1984).

Lapierre, Nicole, *Pensons ailleurs* (Gallimard, 'Folio essais', 2004).

Larbaud, Valery, *An Homage to Jerome: Patron Saint of Translators*, tr. Jean-Paul de Chezet (Marlboro Press, 1984).

Lemaire, Gérard-Georges, *Métamorphoses de Kafka*, exhibition catalogue (Éditions Éric Koehler; Musée du Montparnasse, 2002).

Levi, Primo, *The Drowned and the Saved*, tr. Raymond Rosenthal (Summit Books, 1988).

——, *If This Is a Man and The Truce*, tr. Stuart Woolf (Abacus, 2003).

——, *The Mirror Maker: Stories and Essays*, tr. Raymond Rosenthal (Schocken Books, 1989).

——, *Other People's Trades*, tr. Raymond Rosenthal (Michael Joseph, 1989).
——, *Œuvres* (Robert Laffont, 'Bouquins', 2005).
——, *The Search for Roots: A Personal Anthology*, tr. Peter Forbes (Ivan R. Dee, 2003).
——, *The Voice of Memory: Interviews, 1961–1987*, ed. Marco Belpoliti and Robert Gordon, tr. Robert Gordon (New Press, 2001).
Löwy, Michael, 'Chaînes en papier: Despotisme bureaucratique et servitude volontaire dans Le Château de Franz Kafka', *Diogène*, no. 204 (2003/4).
Mansanti, Céline, *La Revue transition (1927–1938): le Modernisme historique en devenir* (Presses universitaires de Rennes, 2009).
Márai, Sándor, *Ce que j'ai voulu taire*, tr. Catherine Fay (Albin Michel, 2014).
Mason, Eudo C., *Rilke, Europe, and the English-Speaking World* (Cambridge University Press, 1961).
Merleau-Ponty, Maurice, 'Eye and Mind' (1961), tr. Carleton Dallery, in *The Merleau-Ponty Aesthetics Reader: Philosophy and Painting*, ed. Galen A. Johnson and Michael B. Smith (Northwestern University Press, 1993).
Monegal, Emir Rodriguez, *Jorge Luis Borges: A Literary Biography* (E. P. Dutton, 1978).
Montini, Chiara, 'La traduction du *Procès de Kafka*, par Primo Levi, un conflit entre le même et l'autre', in Francesca Manzari and Fridrun Rinner (eds),

Traduire le même, l'Autre et le soi (Presses universitaires de Provence, 2011).

Murat, Laure, *Passage de l'Odéon: Sylvia Beach, Adrienne Monnier et la vie littéraire à Paris dans l'entre-deux-guerres* (Fayard, 2003).

——, *Proust, roman familial* (Robert Laffont, 2023).

Musil, Robert, *Essais: conférences, critique, aphorismes et réflexions*, ed. and tr. Philippe Jaccottet (Seuil, 1984).

——, *The Man Without Qualities*, tr. Sophie Wilkins (Picador, 2017).

Nabokov, Vladimir, *The Gift*, tr. Michael Scammel and Dmitri Nabokov (Penguin, 2001).

——, *Lectures on Literature*, ed. Fredson Bowers (Mariner Books, 2002).

——, *Pnin* (Vintage, 1989).

Nekula, Marek, *Franz Kafka and His Prague Contexts*, tr. Robert Russell and Carly McLaughlin (Karolinum Press, 2016).

Nora, Pierre, *Realms of Memory: Rethinking the French Past*, ed. Lawrence D. Kitzman, tr. Arthur Goldhammer, 3 vols (Columbia University Press, 1996–8).

Nouss, Alexis, 'La Traduction mélancolique (sur Paul Celan)', *TTR: Traduction, Terminologie, Rédaction*, vol. 11, no. 2 (1998).

Ortega y Gasset, 'The Misery and the Splendor of Translation' (1937), tr. Elizabeth Gamble Miller, in Rainer Schulte and John Biguenet (eds), *Theories of*

Translation: An Anthology of Essays from Dryden to Derrida (University of Chicago Press, 1992).

Oustinoff, Michaël, 'Le "sens de la langue" ou la dimension cachée des sens', *Hermès, La Revue*, no. 74 (2016).

Oz, Amos, *A Tale of Love and Darkness*, tr. Nicholas de Lange (Vintage, 2005).

Reznik, Serge, 'L'écriture de la langue', *Che Vuoi?*, no. 26 (2006).

Robert, Marthe, *As Lonely as Franz Kafka*, tr. Ralph Manheim (Schocken Books, 1986).

Roth, Joseph, *Croquis de voyage*, tr. Jean Ruffet (Points, 2016).

Roth, Philip, *The Professor of Desire* (Jonathan Cape, 1978).

——, *Shop Talk: A Writer and His Colleagues and Their Work* (Mariner Books, 2001).

Sartre, Jean-Paul, *Situations*, tr. Benita Eisler (George Braziller, 1965).

Scholem, Gershom, *Le Nom de Dieu et la théorie kabbalistique du langage*, tr. Thomas Piel (Allia, 2018).

——, 'Thoughts about Our Language (1926)', in *On the Possibility of Jewish Mysticism in Our Time and Other Essays*, ed. Avraham Shapira, tr. Jonathan Chipman (Jewish Publication Society, 1997).

Schulz, Bruno, *The Complete Fiction of Bruno Schulz*, tr. Celina Wieniewska (Walker, 1989).

——, *Letters and Drawings of Bruno Schulz, with Selected Prose*, ed. Jerzy Ficowski, tr. Walter

Arndt and Victoria Nelson (Harper and Row, 1988).

Shavit, Zohar, 'Fabriquer une culture nationale: le Rôle des traductions dans la constitution de la littérature hébraïque', *Actes de la recherche en sciences sociales*, no. 144 (2002).

Spector, Scott, *Prague Territories: National Conflict and Cultural Innovation in Kafka's Fin de Siècle* (University of California Press, 2000).

Steiner, George, *After Babel: Aspects of Language and Translation* (Oxford University Press, 1975).

——, *Language and Silence: Essays on Language, Literature, and the Inhuman* (Yale University Press, 1998).

Surya, Michel, 'De Kafka à Slansky: pour une théorie de l'auto-critique', *Lignes*, no. 37 (1999).

Tall, Emily, 'Who Is Afraid of Franz Kafka? Kafka Criticism in the USSR', *Slavic Review*, vol. 35, no. 3 (2017).

Thiesse, Anne-Marie, *La Fabrique de l'écrivain national: entre littérature et politique* (Gallimard, 'Bibliothèque des histoires', 2019).

Thompson, Ralph, 'Books of the Times', *New York Times*, 18 October 1937.

Todorov, Tzvetan, *The Fantastic: A Structural Approach to a Literary Genre*, tr. Richard Howard (Cornell University Press, 1975).

Traynor, Ian, 'Murals Illuminate Holocaust Legacy Row', *Guardian*, 2 July 2001.

Valéry, Paul, *Cahiers*, ed. Judith Robinson, 2 vols (Gallimard, 'Bibliothèque de la Pléiade', 1973).

Veinstein, Léa, *Les philosophes lisent Kafka: Benjamin, Arendt, Anders, Adorno* (Éditions de la Maison des sciences de l'homme, 2019).

Vialatte, Alexandre, *Les Bananes de Königsberg* (Julliard, 1985).

——, *Chroniques de la montagne*, 2 vols (Robert Laffont, 'Bouquins', 2000).

——, *Kafka ou l'innocence diabolique* (Les Belles Lettres, 1998).

——, *Mon Kafka* (Les Belles Lettres, 2010).

Vialatte, Jean, and Paul Paulhan, *Correspondance, 1921–1968*, ed. Denis Wetterwald (Julliard, 1997).

Volovici, Marc, *German as a Jewish Problem: The Language Politics of Jewish Nationalism* (Stanford University Press, 2020).

Wagenbach, Klaus, *Franz Kafka: les années de jeunesse (1883–1912)*, tr. Elisabeth Gaspar (Mercure de France, 1967).

Wagnerová, Alena, *La famille Kafka de Prague*, tr. Nicola Casanova (Grasset, 2004).

Wieviorka, Annette, *The Era of the Witness*, tr. Jared Stark (Cornell University Press, 2006).

Zweig, Stefan, *The World of Yesterday*, tr. Anthea Bell (University of Nebraska Press, 2013).